CONTENTS

Foreword by the Author.............................. 4
My Own Path............................................ 6
Introduction............................................. 7
Appetizers and Starters........................... 20
Soups..................................................... 32
Sauces................................................... 41
Condiments............................................ 49
Salads.................................................... 56
Sides...................................................... 66
Whole Grains.......................................... 92
Potatoes................................................108
Beans and Lentils..................................117
The Quiche............................................121
Meats....................................................125
Poultry...................................................146
Fish and Seafood..................................162
Healthy Recipes for Children.................177
Dinners..................................................181
Desserts................................................188
Breakfast...............................................200
Sources.................................................208
About the Author...................................214

# Foreword by the Author

My goal in writing this book is to share my passion for healthy cooking as well as my knowledge and experience. The result is a comprehensive organic cookbook that is meant to be a hands-on guide that is both simple and fun. I wanted to create a real tool which would actually be useful in terms of planning and preparing foods in your everyday life, while at the same time integrating an organic, healthy lifestyle in an easy way.

All recipes are designed to taste delicious, to be simple and nutritionally balanced. The purpose of this book is to provide you with easy-to-make recipes that will save you time and money by allowing you to prepare your own food and have enough leftovers for additional meals while eating healthier than ever before, all without sacrificing taste. I encourage you to eat complete meals that contain pure natural power for a healthy lifestyle. I promise that if you incorporate these recipes and tips into your diet, it will help you achieve a healthy balance!

# My own path to health

Like many kids, I was a very picky eater and started putting on weight at an early age. I was drawn to the bad stuff and obesity ran in my family. I still remember the very moment that, while taking a bath, I noticed my big, round belly; it really looked like a car tire around my waist. I was about 10 years old, but it wasn't until I was fifteen that I finally made up my mind to do something about it. I began reading about nutrition and started an exercise regimen in my dad's basement, lifting weights.

Progress was very slow at first, but over the next few years, I became more committed to living a healthy lifestyle and joined a gym. I continued to study both nutrition and physical training and took a fitness instructor's course at the age of 19, right before Sweden's mandatory army service took effect. After leaving the army, I continued my education and received a personal trainer diploma from the Swedish National Institute of Sports Education.

Great nutrition goes hand in hand with achieving fitness goals and this inspired me to become more active in the kitchen and cook my own meals. I discovered I had a natural talent and deep passion for cooking. I brought my lunch and snacks to school every day and I didn't miss one meal.

I thought about competing in athletic fitness and I trained very hard to perfect my physique. This brought me to London, where I spent several years working as a personal trainer. I was introduced to a more holistic and organic lifestyle by colleagues and other people I met in the health community. I also earned a diploma in holistic massage as well as completing other nutritional wellness courses. A few years later, I enrolled at Santa Monica College in California where I received an AA. While in Los Angeles, I worked with several catering companies and soon after decided to follow my passion and joined the prestigious Le Cordon Bleu.

The changes I made in my lifestyle, including switching to organic foods, had a huge impact on how I felt, my energy levels and overall well-being and balance. For me, what started as a desire to take control over my health and appearance grew into a complete and healthy lifestyle that I still embody today. It is our own responsibility to eat healthy, stay active and choose to live a good life. I hope my story can inspire you to follow a healthy path with easy-to-prepare organic recipes and by staying active. If I did it, you can do it too!

# Introduction
## How to make it simple in the kitchen:

I do not know how many times I have heard the phrase, "I don't have time" or "It's too hard" to cook and prepare food. Obviously, if you have never been in a kitchen before, it may be difficult to know what you are doing, but it does not have to be. The first rule is to plan ahead so you can do a lot more at the same time by simply putting all tasks in the correct order.

For example, if you are making brown rice and chicken, you should start by boiling the rice while you prepare the chicken as cooking the rice takes more time. This may seem obvious, but it is the most fundamental aspect of saving time while cooking. It ensures that everything is ready at the same time and that nothing is ready prematurely, which can cause some of the food items to either dry out or cool down. The following are some simple rules and step-by-step actions that you can take to optimize your effectiveness in the kitchen:

*1. Clean as you go!* This is the single most important time saver. If you peel an onion, for example, make sure you have a can or bag handy to remove waste immediately.

*2. As soon as you finish using a pot, rinse it out or soak it.* It takes so little time, especially since you are already holding it in your hand. Or pour hot water in the pot to make cleaning later easier. If you wait until you've finished cooking, you will have created a mountain of dishes! This practice will also provide you with a clean and clear workspace throughout the process.

*3. Complete one step at a time.* For example, if you are peeling and chopping potatoes, you would want to complete the step of peeling before chopping. Doing so will save you time since you are not skipping back and forth during the cooking process. Also, complete all of your preparations before starting to cook so you can maintain your timing and not have to look for/prepare an ingredient while you cook.

*4. Start cooking your starches first.* Some starches like rice can usually benefit from sitting to absorb fluids and flavors. Also, have water already boiling if you are making noodles or pasta, so you can simply throw them in the pot when needed. An exception would be if you are cooking meat in the oven for hours.

*5. Preheat the oven.* Preheating the oven before it is to be used will guarantee that you have the right temperature when required.

**6. Make your own marinades**. If you are cooking something that needs to be marinated, make the marinade and let it sit at room temperature while you prepare the rest of the ingredients.

**7. Organize all ingredients for each step.** If the vegetables need preparation, do so first and put them in bowls so that they are ready to be used.

**8. Wait as long as you can to cook meats, fish and poultry.** That will both assure freshness and prevent it from drying out.

**9. Put any spare moments to good use.** For example, one can start a salad, since it simply needs to be tossed, or begin preparing for other dishes' early stages.

## Use what you have

I don't know how many times I have been invited into a kitchen with the statement, "I have NOTHING in the cupboards," and I still ended up cooking a great meal. The key is assessing what you have to work with; obviously, if there really is absolutely nothing in the cupboards, it will be very hard to make a meal. Check if there are any starches in the house such as rice, potatoes, pasta, or even a piece of bread that can be put to use.

If there is no fresh or frozen meat or fish in the fridge, perhaps there is a can of tuna, beans or legumes. Almost any vegetable can be added to a dish that includes starch to make it tastier and more nutritious. Not to mention, it is a great and easy way to add signature to your dish. Scout the cupboards and use your own creativity to try some of the easily personalized recipes below and create a great meal out of 'nothing.'

## Plan ahead; fresh is always better.

I remember reading somewhere that some people, even to this day, only go food shopping about once a month, which will likely result in the major part of what is in their shopping cart being frozen or canned. With the exception of some fish, organic beans and diced tomatoes, almost anything that comes out of a can has very little nutritional value.

The color and flavor of canned goods is often considerably less appealing than fresh. In addition, fresh foods retain life energy, which gives you life energy. Consider one more benefit; lifeless canned vegetables are not as tempting. This is one of the reasons most children are not very interested in vegetables! When buying groceries, make sure they are in their simplest, most raw state. Cook it yourself and cook it just enough so that nothing gets destroyed in the process.

Preparing fresh vegetables is no more difficult or expensive; just chop them up and steam them lightly for a few minutes. Maybe add a little good quality oil or butter and sea salt towards the end and voila! I urge you to put fresh organic vegetables to the test; serve them to children or selective adults and watch for a more positive reaction.

Ideally, shopping should be done about twice to three times a week to so that every item is fresh and of high quality. That is usually how long it takes to consume basic items, so with a little planning, it takes very little time to buy fresh produce and meats. If you find it hard to plan and come up with things to make, rotate your protein sources weekly and shop accordingly.

For instance, make chicken on Monday, beef on Tuesday, fish on Wednesday, vegetarian on Thursday and so on. Never substitute good quality food with 'supplementation' (vitamins, etc.) since these can never replace the nutrition of real food. Break the habit of eating junk food as this will actually be more expensive in the long run, both to your health and your wallet. Simply make sure everything is fresh and organic. A great way to make certain that everything is fresh is to shop at your local farmers markets and health food stores. Minimizing the distance food has to travel has a number of benefits in addition from freshness, which include minimizing toxic by-products (for example, by reducing packaging), fuel consumption and air pollution such as exhaust fumes.

## Keep it simple

Use the recipes in this book to create your weekly menu. Eat 3 solid meals per day, breakfast, lunch, dinner, and at the same time each day—for example, breakfast between 8-9 am, lunch from 12-2 pm and dinner around 7-8 pm. The more regular your food intake, the better your body is able to utilize food and regulate elimination. Always stock up on supplies that have a long shelf life, brown rice, potatoes, quinoa, etc., so you always have them available and ready to use.

## Equipment and Methods

### *Steaming:*
Steaming is a great method of cooking vegetables as well as some meats and fish since the process requires little to no additional fat to cook and the vitamins remain. Do not throw away the water that is left in the pot; it is great for making your stock, which will increase its nutritional value as well as flavor. If you do not have a steamer, use a stainless steel strainer and put it in a pot with a little water in the bottom, place the vegetables on top and cover with a lid.

*Baking Dish:*
As with steaming, using an ovenproof baking dish is an excellent and easy way to cook your vegetables and proteins to induce many nuances of flavor. The possibilities for variations are endless. Slow cooking preserves the nutritional value of the food and concentrates flavors. Simply mix all your ingredients in the baking dish, add spices and oil and put it in the oven. A small amount of water can be added so that the food stays moist. If you notice that the food is getting too much color, just cover it with some aluminum foil.

*The Grill Pan:*
Regardless of whether you have an outdoor grill or just an oven grill pan, grilling is always a great way to cook; it is easy and gives other dimensions of flavor. You usually do not need any extra fat for cooking; just be certain that the grill is really hot before you put the food on it. In regards to meat, it is ready to turn when it no longer sticks to the surface. Trying to turn too soon will result in the meat tearing. Never put oil directly on a grill pan as this will create excessive smoke. Alternately, a thin coat of oil or a marinade can be added to the meat before grilling.

*Sauté or Pan Fry:*
Pan frying and/or sautéing is one of your best friends in the kitchen because it is easy as well as a great way to blend flavors. Just make sure the pans are of high quality, such as stainless steel or titanium. Avoid coated non-stick surfaces as these scratch easily and leach into your food. Cast iron pans with thick bottoms will retain heat far better while spreading it more evenly and so are more suitable for cooking meat and cooking in general.

*Pots:*
This cookware is used for steaming and boiling as well as making sauces and casseroles. Just be sure they are of the same quality as the cookware mentioned above and that you have different sizes to accommodate all your needs.

*Braising:*
The best way to get melting soft meat out of a tough cut is to slowly braise it for hours, preferably in a good Dutch oven casserole pot for even heat distribution. I like to keep the temperature fairly low, around 275°F - 325°F. That gives the meat time for the connective tissues to break down. If braised at too high of a temperature, the meat will tend to be dry even though it is submerged in a liquid.

*Knives:*
As long as you have good knives in the kitchen, food preparation and cooking will be far more enjoyable. You can improvise with most other utensils and tools but not with knives. It is not only difficult, but actually dangerous to work with dull knifes. Because of the additional pressure required to make effective

use of a dull knife, you are more likely to cut yourself. This is less of a potential hazard with a sharp knife since there is less chance of slipping. If you have not done so already, toss out your old knives. Buy at least one or two top quality 'high carbon content' knifes to accompany you in your culinary adventures.

### Food Processor:
A good food processor can be your biggest time saver in the kitchen as it can blend and chop everything from nuts, seeds, fruit and vegetables to make sauces, soups, juices and more.

### Spatulas and Containers:
These are essential tools for stirring and multiple tasks; choose a variety of spatulas with different shapes and forms. Stick to natural materials such as wood or stainless steel. Avoid plastic as much as possible as plastic may leach into your food and leave a horrible taste as well as unwanted chemicals. If you must use plastic while preparing food, make sure it is heat resistant and appropriate for the purpose for which you are using it. This also includes plastic storage containers. Instead, use glass as much as possible when storing foods since no leaching occurs and glass is more efficient at keeping the air out, allowing your food to stay fresher longer.

## The Good Food and Health Pointers:

In this book, there are numerous recipes that offer delicious flavor and color combinations that have a healthy, balanced ratio of fat, proteins and carbohydrates. Food should not be a chore, either in preparing or eating. It should be joy to create and pleasing to share. Eating healthy will not only increase your effectiveness, but also your motivation and energy. Junk food, as you may know, might be comforting for the moment, but harmful in the long run. When you have changed the way you nourish your body, it will actually start to let you know what kind of foods are good for you and therefore naturally help you to avoid those that are not.

You know you will need lunch, so start to think about planning it rather than just allowing it to happen. Without real food energy, you can count on heading straight to the coffee pot, or resorting to sugary snacks just to try to make it through the rest of the day. Any 'energy' you get from such non-nutritional sources will not last long, resulting in a crash. Do not eat too much at lunch (or any meal) since your body cannot utilize and digest too much food at one time. This will also result in your feeling sluggish.

Also, any excess energy that you put in your body is likely to make you fat, regardless of the source. As a general rule, portions of starch and protein should be no larger than the size of your fist. The rest of the plate can be filled with fresh vegetables and topped with fresh unrefined oil for added benefit. Below are basic yet highly effective pointers on how to incorporate a healthy food and lifestyle regime:

*1. Listen to thy body: find your metabolic type.*

Everybody is different and so are their energy needs. There is a reason why we have a built-in system of 'feeling like' having a certain food. Unfortunately, today most people have disrupted this built-in ability to recognize what the body actually needs by eating too much processed and highly addictive food. The best way to get back in tune with the body is to clean up your diet and mentally monitor each plate of food eaten. Start with eliminating most of the carbohydrates in each meal, and slowly increase the portion size of carbohydrates by increments.

There are two extremes of preferred 'fuel' ratio:
1) some people do very well with a high carbohydrate intake and a low fat and protein ratio—we can refer to "Weight Watchers" here—and 2) the other extreme are people who do better with a high protein and fat ratio, yet very little carbohydrates, also known as the "Atkins Diet." The reality is that most people fall somewhere along this spectrum, so the only real way to find your perfect fuel ratio is to experiment by introducing carbohydrates in increments. Optimally, after having a meal, you should be satisfied, content and full with energy for hours without feeling the need for a sugar or caffeine boost. If you feel hungry or just feel like a pick-me-up, have small snacks in between meals. Fresh fruit is detoxifying and regenerating but should be combined with fat and/or protein (cheese or nuts, for example) to balance the sugar and slow the absorption process.

The most essential element in fine tuning your own personal diet regime is finding balance. Always have a meal ratio that is proportionate and experiment to find the right "fuel ratio" between the carbohydrates, protein and fats. This practice is also referred to as the "Metabolic Typing Diet." Generally, the type of food you are most attracted to, say, after a workout, can give you valuable insight on how start to fine tune your food source ratios. If more attracted to fat, eat more protein and fats in relation to carbohydrates. If you are more attracted to carbohydrates, eat a little less fat but keep the protein high.

*2. Honor your meal times.*
There is a common saying that you should eat small and often, which is true enough, but the key is to not use that as an excuse to constantly chow down on food. After a meal or a snack, you should wait at least 3 hours before eating anything at all. There are adverse effects of constantly stimulating secretion of insulin, which happens even with small amounts of food. Reviewing some of the primary reasons, every time your body releases insulin, your body automatically goes into "fat-storing mode"—therefore, everything eaten after or during (especially if the energy is not needed) will be stored as fat. Another top reason is that if your body constantly releases insulin, you may disrupt the pancreas' ability to produce it, which may lead to diabetes. Respect your

meal times and stick to your meal routine. Try to eliminate continuous intake of drinks that contain little or no nutritional value, i.e., juice, soda, sports drinks etc. These can interrupt a natural and necessary process that occurs every time your stomach has completed a digestive cycle, a "flush" of the colon that aids digestion and regulates elimination.

Also, with a constant input of juice, for example, you are triggering insulin exertion to keep your sugar levels under control. That is why and when the body starts to decrease its fat-burning properties and starts to store the body fat instead. Eat larger meals earlier in the day as you will use the energy throughout the day. Eat less in the evening when you will not be using the energy. Think of your food intake pattern as an inverted triangle in which the biggest meals are early in the day and the smaller in the evening. However, if you have a work-out in the afternoon, make sure you have a complete evening meal. Do not eat anything 2-3 hours prior to bedtime. If you are very hungry in the evening, have a small portion of a slow-release protein source like casein, which is derived from milk and can be found in cottage cheese, for example. It is also available in protein powder

### 3. Another note on water.
We all know to drink a lot of water as the general diet experts have told us for years, and it is worth re-mentioning that keeping hydrated during the day is one of the most important factors for maintaining health. We are 70% water, and even a drop of 1% in fluids will decrease our functionality by 10%—not to mention the numerous functions in the body that are directly dependent upon proper hydration. The one thing I want to address here is fluids while eating. You should drink a big glass or two of clean water, not tap water, 15 minutes before the meal and not so much during. The reason for this is that if you drink too much water while eating, you will dilute your digestive fluids, resulting in poorer digestion and nutritional absorption. Also it is a good idea to drink hot fluids, as cold fluids solidify the fat in the food and may end up clogging your system.

### 4. Fear not the fat, but the sugar.
How many times have you heard "but it is fat-free and therefore healthy," with no mention that you will instead consume a ton of sugar? We need good quality fats in our diet for several reasons . . . here are a few: the immune system's functionality, protection of the brain and its functions, and the absorption of the fat solvable vitamins A and D. Sugar, on the other hand, is not only useless as an energy source and contains mere empty calories, it also leaches calcium from the bones and other vitamins and minerals from the cells, not to mention its obvious weight-gaining tendencies. Craving sugar every day in any shape or form? Then you are addicted to sugar, which is proven to be more addictive than heroin! Considering the fact that sugar has become cheap, it finds its way into most foods and often in the form of a high fructose corn syrup (which is even worse as that also is cancerogenic). Pay close attention to your food sources and eliminate processed, pre-packaged foods. Go cold turkey and ride out the wave, which may last a week to ten days. After that, you will have a much more stable energy level throughout the day!

### 5. Pursue meal and snack balance.
Also related to food ratio is the importance of a macronutrient balance for each meal, meaning the balance between proteins, carbohydrates and fats. All three of these macronutrients should be represented in every meal or snack to assure proper energy and nutritional absorption. You need the carbohydrates to absorb the protein, preventing its use as energy as, optimally, it is used as building blocks. You need the fat to balance the meal and its glycemic index, as it lowers the value of the meal, resulting in longer lasting energy without the classic sugar crash. You need protein in every meal for the enzymatic processes of the body and its role in maintaining strength of muscle mass.

Save treats for the weekend. Doing so will make you appreciate them when you do have them. Also, by eating good food for the most of the week, the negative effects of 'treats' will not be nearly as great. It can also serve as motivation to make healthy choices.

To detoxify your body, choose green vegetables and whole grain foods, as these contain a much richer spectrum of nutrients and fibers to help you assimilate and digest the foods. The greens will also make your body more alkaline, counteracting blood acidity, which is an unfortunate reality for most people that causes a toxic effect on the body and its functions. Avoid white processed food and refined grains, as these are less nutritional.

If you have a sensation of discomfort or "nausea" during the initial period of switching from junk food to healthy eating habits, be patient! When your body detoxifies, the toxins released go into your blood stream and can make you feel ill. This is only temporary, so it is important to not give up and fall into bad habits.

### 6. Learn the importance of organic.
This topic could be a book in itself, but I will outline the most significant reasons. First and foremost, organic means the food is chemical-, pesticide-, fungicide- and hormone-free. If foods are produced using any of these elements, they will end up in that food and you will eat them. The body does not recognize any of these substances as food and they will get stored in your body, year after year. This is possibly one of the main sources of diseases today.

Furthermore, when food is produced with the use of these chemicals, the process is faster and kills naturally occurring microbes in the earth—which are responsible for giving the food its nutrition—leaving you with an already dead food that is stripped of its nutritional value.

You need great quality raw materials to build and fuel your body. Without those materials, not only will you have to eat twice as much to get adequate nutrition, you are also more susceptible to reaching for the crappy stimulation food items because you are simply not fed properly. All the excess calories that you will have to consume to accommodate for the lack of nourishment will get stored as fat. Another important factor is to vary what you eat as your body can become allergic or sensitive to basically anything that is consumed in excess. Consuming foods in small amounts and more sporadically will minimize the risk of allergies and food sensitivity.

### *7. Avoid fast and processed foods.*
The advance of fast and processed foods is indeed a product of our fast-moving society, where there is simply no longer time to cook. However, the faster a food is, the faster it will take you to your grave, literally. The lack of nutrients and the supremely poor ingredients of fast and prepackaged foods will not only make you gain weight, they will also most certainly make you sick. I can't stress enough the importance of making your own food in order to know what's in it. Plan ahead for the week, make bigger batches of food and bring your lunch with you each day; that will save both time and money. That little extra effort will be well worth it in the long run!

### *8. You shall not be deceived: the microwave is not your best friend.*
Most people like the convenience and speed of the microwave, but from a nutritional standpoint, it absolutely kills the food. Microwave radiation causes the food to heat up by vibrating the water molecules in the food; hence, it often comes out unevenly cooked as some parts of the food contain more water than other parts. However, this radiation also breaks down the actual food molecules, effectively killing the nutrients and leaving you with a dead food with vastly less nutritional value. You can also clearly detect a loss of flavor. Now, if the food that you are microwaving also happens to be pre-packed and frozen, you can rest assured that you have a minus on the nutritional value of that meal! Make the effort to heat up your food conventionally or eat it cold.

### *9. Don't kill the coffee, just the sugar.*
There is a lot of conflicting information on coffee and caffeinated beverages in general. Actually, a small amount of coffee a day is completely defendable as it stimulates your metabolism and helps burn more fat during your daily routine. There are also studies that suggest that a moderate intake of coffee decreases the risk of heart disease. The main thing to be aware of here is two-fold: One, where does your coffee come from and how is it produced? Coffee companies frequently spray a ton of pesticides on the coffee that you end up drinking. It also tends to be heavily processed, which further decreases the level of naturally occurring antioxidants found in natural coffee. Two, what else comes in your coffee drink? If it is an extra-large Frappuccino with 50 grams of sugar and whipped cream and chocolate on top, it is not coffee anymore; it's a dessert with a caloric value equivalent to half a day's worth of energy from healthy foods. Have your coffee with minimal additives and if you must sweeten, use stevia.

### *10. Avoid gluten at all costs.*
More and more people are found to have gluten intolerance, also known as celiac disease. In my opinion, gluten should be avoided as much as possible, which is not easy as it finds its way into most processed foods. Once in a while, it's fine to consume gluten, but if it occurs on a daily basis, a number of things happen in the body. First of all, gluten is most commonly consumed

in any form of white bread, which, considering its glycemic value, is actually as bad as eating pure white sugar. Second and more importantly, when gluten is consumed and digested, it forms a lining not too different from glue in our digestive tract. We have micro hairs in our digestive system, or villi, that collect the broken down nutrients directly from the intestines. The gluten effectively clogs these hairs and leads to an array of problems, including lack of nutritional absorption, as well as colon infections and constipation. There are alternative options to bread and gluten products like sprouted rye bread, quinoa and other gluten-free options.

### *11. Consider the color of your food.*
Always be sure to have greens and colors on your plate due to their vital anti-oxidants, vitamins and trace minerals, without which your body cannot function optimally. The more color a food has, the healthier it is and is surely more pleasing to the eye. Fresh foods retain life energy and have naturally present enzymes that aid digestion and the absorption of other nutrients.

### *12. Get to bed on time.*
Get to bed on time! Your body's physical repair process occurs most effectively between the hours of 10pm - 2am at night. These hours of sleep are the most important. The more regular of a routine you have, the better for your body.

## Nutrients

### *Fats*
Eating fat does not make you fat. Our bodies need fat for the healthy function of many organs and systems: the brain, immune system, heart and skin. What should be restricted are the saturated fats found in animal products; note that I said 'restricted,' not 'excluded.' If the products are organic and free range, the fat will be of far greater quality. Remember, it is not just the amount of fat but the quality that counts. What should definitely be avoided are 'trans fats' and 'hydrogenated oils' (gas injected for a mere 'emulsion effect') that are found in most processed foods and also in so called 'healthy' and 'balance your cholesterol' fats and spreads. These fats are more similar to plastic than to food in their chemical structure and can damage your body since it does not recognize these as a food. Toxins are often present in the fat of conventional food so it is best to avoid wherever possible. Feel free to use olive oil, sunflower oil, avocado, fatty (if possible, caught wild) fish like salmon, sea bass or mackerel, fish oils, nuts and seeds since these are packed with essential fatty acids.

### *Protein*
Protein is another essential macronutrient that is necessary for the rebuilding of cells as well as bodily systems such as hormonal, enzymatic and more. The most complete protein can be found in meats, fish, poultry, eggs and dairy. You can substitute animal protein with beans, lentils and other legumes which contain protein; however, some of the amino acids are missing and you would need to combine these foods with appropriate grains for the protein to be complete. Protein is one of the nutrients that must be added to the body through whole food in order for it to function properly, as it cannot produce protein itself.

*Carbohydrates*
Carbohydrates are fuel for the body; the brain requires carbohydrates in the form of glucose to function. With this in mind, it is important that the carbohydrate be from a wholesome source. Whole grains are an excellent source of quality carbohydrates that are also low on the glycemic index (a measurement of how fast carbohydrates increase blood sugar levels) so the energy gained from the carbohydrates will be longer lasting. Slow release carbohydrates are also found in vegetables. Wholesome carbohydrate sources contain the important fibers and other digestive enzymes that we need to process our foods efficiently.

## Some words on exercise and movement

There are more aspects to health than eating habits and one of them are the habit of movement. In this modern world of instant communication and digital networking, people are becoming more and more sedentary. Keep in motion. Make movement a part of your daily life, as it is a key element of keeping healthy. I'm sure you have heard how important exercise and movement is to maintaining a healthy body. The key is to make exercise interesting and fun. Enjoy the movement by making it into something that you would actually not want to miss out on for anything. We are physically designed for movement. True imbalances occur when we do not provide the body with this natural exposure to exercise and movement.

Find your individual way to movement, even if that simply means just walking more often, or taking the stairs instead to the elevator. Use all the opportunities you have to move in your daily life. Remember what you thought was fun when you were young and bring it back into your life. For example; running/jogging, hiking, swimming, cycling, skating, sports, lifting weights or even dancing. 20 minutes a day can be sufficient and we all have 20 minutes somewhere in the day. No energy? You may be surprised to find that when you change your diet and start to move, little by little, progressively, the energy will come back and tenfold. You actually lose a lot of energy when you do not include movement on a daily basis. It also helps you to maintain healthy circulation, which increases your metabolism, actually giving you more energy.

You may have heard the saying "The less I do, the less I get done"? This concept is the same in relation to movement. As you gain the momentum of movement in your daily life, you will naturally have more energy to do everything else in your life because you have increased your effectiveness. This lifestyle includes many additional benefits such as improving circadian rhythms, getting rid of addictions, timed bowel function and generally maintaining homeostasis of the body.

## Organic versus non-organic foods

These days, the quality of our food is vastly deteriorating while the quantity that we consume is increasing. Improper and insufficient nutrition is becoming more and more of a fact in modern society. As obesity increases, declining health is at an all-time high. Due to the amount of chemicals used and the way that the food is processed, this is ultimately leading to a rapid decline in general health. Our ancestors rarely faced these problems because everything they consumed was pure and in its natural state. The importance for food to be of an organic standard is critical. The best way to ascertain that your food is organic is to get certified organic products from a reputable company such as Horizon Organics and/or Organic Valley.

Although the media sometimes gives a different impression, organic food has proven health benefits. Very few people are conscious of the benefits of organic food and the potential harmful effects of non-organic food. What you eat will influence numerous functions of your body, including cell regeneration and repair.

Besides the 'energy giving' macronutrients, protein, carbohydrate and fat, organic food provides both a full range and a specific combination of nutritional elements and nutrients that are essential for survival. Most of these nutrients can be acquired from food but to provide maximum nutritional content, the source should be organic. We are designed to eat foods that are in a pure natural state and do not contain chemicals, herbicides, pesticides, etc. However, the food that we're generally exposed to is so processed that our bodies barely even recognize it as food, resulting in all those non-food elements getting stored in the body. The lack of necessary nutrients make it inadequate to fuel our bodies and gain optimal health. Most produce, if conventionally grown, has a nutrient value that is so low that a person would likely have to eat twice the amount, inducing side effects. Eating in this manner causes the body to be lacking in nutrients; it will respond by creating sugar cravings and/or cravings for caffeine or other stimulants, bingeing or generally not 'being satisfied.'

How many advertisements have you seen lately that state that a particular pill works like magic to help you lose weight, lower your high cholesterol or in other ways improve your health. I find it interesting that our priorities have been reduced to the notion that a 'magic pill' will solve all of our health problems. To use an analogy: A man notices that one of the trees in his garden has turned brown and withered. He calls a gardener who comes over to have a look and gives product advice. The man goes to the store and when he acquires the recommended product, he notices that it is merely green paint. This suggests that the gardener recommended that if the brown color of the tree is a problem, then simply paint it green. This analogy symbolizes that as long as a symptom is eliminated, the problem is solved, instead of considering the root cause of that problem in order to correct it. There simply are no magic pills or supplements that can replace good, wholesome, quality food eaten in appropriate (frequent) intervals and amounts. Health benefits are even derived from sharing good food with the right people.

**The difference between organically and conventionally produced foods**
The 'Organic Standard' is based on farming with limited use of chemical pesticides, with the product being free from the involvement of chemical use and or any other processing agent, after or during any part of the production.

Recently, there has been a boom in the popularity of organic food and this has led to many companies 'jumping on board' to make money. Unfortunately, there are ways to get around organic certification that allow companies to label foods as organic without having the farm go through required 3-year 'reset period' from pesticides. When pesticides and other chemical agents are involved in the production of plants, there are a number of different processes that differ from those used in organic farming. Farming conventionally creates a shortfall in the mineral and nutrient ratio that is considered essential for the food to be viewed as whole.

Humans have been involved in agriculture for over 6000 years, but only during the last 50 have we introduced chemical fertilizers and pesticides to 'enhance' the farming procedure. The reason for the usage of fertilizers and pesticides is normally to increase crop production, despite the fact that this is not necessarily true; research has shown that we can eliminate pesticide use by up to 65% without sacrificing crop yields or quality. This information should make us reconsider the widespread use of inorganic fertilizers and pesticides and concern ourselves with its damaging effects and costs on society.

*Health benefits of organic food*

Switching to organic food induces a series of health benefits. Just by eliminating the large number of chemicals used in the production and processing of conventional food, we obtain a positive change in our body's ability to function; if chemical input is minimized, the related diseases can be eliminated to a great extent.

- You will be more satisfied when you eat, eliminating, for example, sweet cravings.
- You will have more energy.
- It tastes better.
- It is better for the environment.

Since what we eat directly corresponds to what we are, it is very important for the food to be of high quality if you want to be of high quality. Would it not be better to live in a world as nature intended?

All of the recipes in this book should be prepared exclusively with organic ingredients. Essentially, all ingredients from produce to meat are available organic; just read the labels and make sure they are certified. The quality in terms of flavor, nutritional value, richness of color and texture is significantly greater in organic food. I have not put 'use organic' before every ingredient as I am explicitly stating it here. Any unusual or non-standard item is listed in the sources section. Please refer to that for detailed information.

# Appetizers and Starters

# Oven Baked Cremini Mushrooms Filled with Herb Aioli

### Serves 8-10

- 1 lb. of cremini mushrooms
- 3 garlic cloves
- 2 cups mayonnaise
- 1 can of artichoke hearts
- ½-1 cup grated Parmesan
- 2 tbsp. dried mixed herbs
- Sea salt and freshly ground black pepper

Preheat the oven to 375°F. In a food processor, start by processing the garlic. Run a spatula along the sides of the bowl, add the other ingredients except the Parmesan and pulse until the artichokes are chopped fairly coarse. Add the Parmesan and pulse until blended.

Use a paper towel to remove dirt from the surfaces of the mushrooms. Scoop out the stem of the mushroom and use a piping bag or teaspoon to fill each mushroom with the mixture. Place the filled mushrooms on a baking sheet and bake for 10-15 min until soft but not falling apart.

# Stuffed Cherry Tomatoes

## Serves 6-8

*20 cherry tomatoes*

Olive and goats cheese filling:
- Scant cup soft goat's cheese
  ⅓ cup finely chopped pitted black olives
- 1-2 cup olive oil
- 1 pressed garlic clove
- 2 tbsp. fresh thyme
- Sea salt and freshly ground black pepper

OR

Artichoke and anchovies filling:
- 1 can of artichoke hearts
- 50 g of anchovies in olive oil
- 8-10 pimiento stuffed olives
- 4-5 tbsp. mayonnaise
- 2 tbsp. crème fraiche (optional)
- Sea salt and freshly ground black pepper

Cut the top of the tomatoes and remove seeds, etc. with a tea spoon or a small melon baller. Turn the tomatoes upside down and place on a piece of kitchen towel to dry.

To make the goat's cheese filling, mix the olives with the garlic and thyme. Blend in the cheese then add some olive oil.

To make the artichoke and anchovies filling, place all ingredients in a food processor and blend until desired thickness is achieved, then add salt and pepper to taste.

Use a pastry bag to fill up each tomato with the selected filling. If you do not have access to a pastry bag, a teaspoon can be used to fill up the tomatoes, but it will not look as nice. Store them cold until ready to serve.

# Sun-dried Tomato and Artichoke Munchies

**Serves 10**

- 10-12 pieces of sliced sprouted bread
- 1 tub of crème fraiche
- 1 small jar of sun-dried tomatoes in oil or marinade
- 2 cans of artichoke hearts
- 1 bag mozzarella cheese
- Sea salt and freshly ground black pepper

Chop the sun-dried tomatoes into small pieces and put them in a bowl with the crème fraiche. Blend in the salt and pepper (to taste) with a fork until the crème fraiche turns slightly red. If you want a lower fat version, you can replace some of the crème fraiche with yogurt. Keep the bowl in the fridge for at least 10 min. to allow the flavors to merge.

Meanwhile, cut the artichoke in four pieces and put them aside. Pre-toast the bread slightly for a crunchier quality, cut them in fours as well and put the pieces on a foil-covered baking tray. Take the crème batter out and with a tablespoon, put a spoonful on each bread piece. Take a piece of the artichoke and place it gently on top of the batter.

Finish off with a sprinkle of mozzarella and bake them (high rack) in the oven on 375°F for about 20 min. They are ready when the cheese is browned. Arrange them nicely on a plate

# Slivers of Pork Tenderloin On Brochette with Horseradish Cream

### Serves 8-10

- 1 cooked whole roasted pork tenderloin with black pepper crust, room temp (See index.)
- 1 French baguette
- Olive oil A/N
- Dried oregano A/N
- 1 cup whipping cream
- 1-2 tbsp. fresh horseradish
- Sea salt and freshly ground black pepper

Preheat the oven to 350°F. Slice the baguette fairly thin on a diagonal. Place on a baking sheet in a single layer and drizzle with olive oil, followed by salt, pepper and oregano.

Roast for 7-10 min., checking frequently as they burn easily. When somewhat browned and crisp, remove from oven and let cool.

Whip the cream fairly hard and add the horseradish and salt and pepper. Taste to check the seasoning. Place a very thin sliver of the pork tenderloin on each brochette and top with a dollop of the cream. Arrange nicely on a platter and serve.

# Pear And Brie Quesadilla Served with Cumin Crème Fraiche

**Serves 8-10**

For quesadilla:
- 6 Bosc pears, peeled, cored and thinly sliced
- ½ wheel of good quality brie, thinly sliced
- 8-10 large flour tortillas

For cumin crème fraiche:
- 1 cup crème fraiche
- 2 tsp. cumin
- 2 tbsp. lemon juice
- Sea salt and freshly ground black pepper to taste

On each tortilla, place the sliced pear in a circle, followed by the brie on top. Top with another tortilla and put in a spray-coated large frying pan. Turn over once when slightly browned.

Cut into 8 pieces and arrange on a platter. For the cumin crème fraiche, combine the ingredients and put a dollop on each tortilla slice.

# Roasted Pepper Salad

**Serves 4-6**

- 1 orange pepper
- 2 red peppers
- 2 yellow peppers
- 4 cloves of garlic, chopped
- 2 tbsp. mixed herbs, oregano, basil and thyme
- 1 pinch of chopped chili peppers (optional)
- A drizzle of olive oil
- Sea salt

Begin by cutting off the bottom part of the peppers, then cut them in half vertically, remove the white pith and slice them into 1 by 2 inch rectangular pieces. Put all ingredients on a baking tray that has been lightly coated with olive oil. Add the spices and drizzle olive oil over the peppers.

Bake in the middle of the oven at 375°F for 20-30 min, or until browned. About half way through the cooking process, turn the peppers over in the pan, using a spatula. Let them cool and serve as a starter or side vegetable dish.

# Foie Gras Creme on Rye Toast with Pickle

**Serves 8-10**

- 1 ½ cup of foie gras or other pate'
- ½ to ¾ cup crème fraiche
- Small pickles sliced lengthwise
- Thin rye bread cut into rounds and lightly toasted
- Sea salt and freshly ground black pepper to taste

With a fork, blend the foie gras and crème fraiche and add salt and pepper to taste. Place mixture in a piping bag and pipe a dollop into the center of each rye round. Place a half pickle on top and present nicely on a platter.

---

# Parmesan Wafers with Tomato Confit

**Serves 6-8**

For the Parmesan wafers:
- 12 tbsp. grated Parmesan
- 2 ½ tbsp. flour
- 3 tbsp. butter, softened
- 1 tsp. freshly ground black pepper

For the tomato topping:
- 4 -5 medium tomatoes, multi-color or heirloom if desired, cut into ¼ inch cubes
- 2-3 tbsp. olive oil
- 2 tbsp. fresh basil, thinly sliced
- 1 tbsp. fresh thyme, chopped
- Sea salt and freshly ground black pepper to taste

Preheat the oven to 400°F. Combine the ingredients for the wafers and knead into a dough. Roll it into an even 4 inch roll. Cut into about 1 ⅛ inch thick pieces. Press them out slightly using your fingers and form into a thin disc. Place all discs with some space in between on a baking sheet lined with a slipmat or parchment paper. Bake in the oven for about 8-10 min until golden brown and sizzling, turning the pan halfway.

Let cool completely then place on paper towels to absorb excess grease. Cut the tomatoes, toss with a little salt and place in a strainer for 20 min. to release and remove some of the water. Place the tomatoes in a mixing bowl and add the remaining ingredients. Let macerate for 10 min. then place a small amount in the center of each wafer and serve.

# Mini Chicken Skewers

### Serves 6-8

- 1½ lbs. chicken breast fillet
- 2 red onions cut into cloves (8 pieces each)
- 4 Portobello mushrooms cut into 8 pieces
- 2 peppers cut into 1-inch rectangles

Marinade:
- 2 cloves pressed garlic
- 1-2 tbsp. soy sauce
- 4 tsp. paprika
- 1 tsp. garlic powder
- tbsp. olive oil
- Sea salt and freshly ground black pepper

To make the marinade, mix the garlic and spices with the soy sauce and slowly add the olive oil while whisking. Cut the chicken breast fillets into small pieces, put them in the marinade and soak for preferably an hour or overnight.

Prepare the onion, mushrooms and peppers and cut them into fairly small pieces. Take wooden or metal skewer pins and divide them in half to get an appetizer size, thread on the chicken and vegetables on the skewers in layers. Put everything in a casserole dish and broil at the top part of the oven, turning occasionally.

The skewers can be cooked in the frying pan or on the grill as well. Alternatively you can omit the vegetables.

# Spicy Tuna Tartar in Cucumber Cup

## Serves 6-8

- 1 lb. sushi grade ahi tuna
- 1-2 jalapeno peppers, or Thai for a spicier tuna
- 1 tbsp. fresh ginger, grated
- 1 garlic clove, minced
- 3 tbsp. sesame oil
- 1-2 tbsp. canola oil
- 1 tbsp. rice vinegar
- 2 tsp. tamari or other light soy sauce
- 1 tsp. lemon juice
- 3 tbsp. toasted sesame seeds
- ½ bunch cilantro, finely chopped
- 1 straight English cucumber

Add the peppers, garlic and ginger in a bowl, followed by the vinegar and lemon juice. Whisk while adding the oils and, lastly, the cilantro and sesame seeds. Cut the tuna into small cubes and add to the dressing.

Let marinade while preparing the cucumber. Peel the cucumber and cut into roughly 1 inch pieces. Scoop out the seeds using a melon baller. Fill each cucumber cup with the tuna and sprinkle some sesame seeds on top.

Alternative presentations are on a fried wonton crisp or a square piece of nori rolled into a cone.

# Soups

A good soup is comforting as well as a great starter to the meal. Enjoy hot soup in cold weather and cold soup when it is warm. Here are a few recipes that are easy to create.

# Shrimp Soup

### Serves 4-6

- 1-2 cups of cooked bay shrimp
- 1 large grated carrot
- 1 cup of soft cream cheese
- 4-6 cups vegetable stock
- 1 cup of crème fraiche
- 1 cup of chopped dill
- 2 cups of filtered water
- 1 tbsp. butter
- Juice of ½ lemon
- Sea salt and freshly ground black pepper

Sauté the carrot in butter; add the stock, cheese and crème fraiche. Let simmer on low temperature for 10 min.

Then add the chopped dill, lemon juice and let sit for another 3 min. To finish, add the shrimp just long enough for them to warm up; otherwise, they will turn rubbery.

# Butternut Squash Soup

## Serves 6-8

- 1 large butternut squash, peeled, cored and coarsely chopped into cubes
- 2 med. russet potatoes, peeled and cut into equal sized cubes
- 2 med. yellow onions, coarsely chopped
- 1 leek, rinsed and coarsely chopped
- 1 garlic clove, chopped
- Knob of butter
- Chicken stock A/N
- ½ cup cream
- Sea salt and freshly ground black pepper to taste

Start by sautéing the onions and leek gently in a pot with the butter. When translucent, add the garlic and cook for another 1-2 min. Add the squash and cook for 3-5 min., stirring occasionally, then add the potatoes and fill the pot with chicken stock until just covered. If you don't have chicken stock, water can be used.

Cover and simmer until the squash and potatoes are soft (15-20 min.). Season with salt and pepper, add the cream and stir. Let cool slightly, then run the soup in batches in a blender. Taste for salt and pepper and garnish with your favorite chopped fresh herbs like parsley.

# Zucchini Mint Soup

**Serves 4-6**

- 6 zucchini, rinsed, ends cut and chopped coarsely
- 3 med. russet potatoes, peeled and cut into equal size cubes that are smaller than the zucchini
- 1 large yellow onion
- Knob of butter
- Vegetable stock A/N
- Pinch ground cumin
- ½ - 1 cup Greek yogurt
- 1 bunch of fresh mint
- Sea salt and white pepper to taste

Sauté the onions in the butter with a pinch of salt. When translucent, add the cumin and stir. Add the zucchini and potatoes and fill the pot with the stock until the vegetables are just covered with liquid.

Cover the pot and simmer for 10-15 min. until the vegetables are soft. Let cool slightly, then add the yogurt, mint and salt and pepper. Puree in batches, stir it all together and taste for mint and the other seasoning. Serve with chopped mint on top.

# White Bean and Tomato Soup

**Serves 4-6**

- 2 cans garbanzo beans, rinsed
- 2 yellow onions
- 3 carrots, peeled and coarsely chopped
- 2 garlic cloves, sliced
- 6 oz. tomato paste
- 1 tsp. cumin
- 1 tsp. coriander
- 1 tsp. celery seed
- 1 bay leaf
- 6 cups of chicken stock
- 1 dollop of cream
- Juice of 1 lemon
- Sea salt and freshly ground black pepper to taste

Sauté the onions in some oil for a few minutes, then add the carrots followed by the garlic. Add the spices and stir until aromatic. Add the tomato paste and cook for another minute while stirring. Add the chicken stock, cover and simmer until the carrots are soft.

Take the pot off the heat, remove the bay leaf, and add the rest of the ingredients. Puree in batches and taste for salt and pepper.

# Vegetable Soup

**Serves 4-6**

- 1 yellow onion, finely chopped
- 2-3 carrots, cut into equal size small cubes
- 3 celery ribs, cut into equal size small cubes
- Knob of butter
- 2 Yukon gold potatoes, cut into the same size as the vegetables
- 6-8 cups of chicken or vegetable stock
- 3 sprigs fresh thyme
- 1 bay leaf
- Sea salt and freshly ground black pepper to taste
- 2 cooked and pulled chicken breasts (optional)

Sauté the onion in the butter with some salt until softened, add the carrots and cook for a few more minutes. Add the thyme and bay leaf and stir. Add the rest of the ingredients except for the optional chicken, cover and simmer until soft.

When done, remove the herbs, add the chicken if desired and taste for salt and pepper.

# Cauliflower and Root Vegetable Soup

**Serves 4-6**

- 1 head of cauliflower, cut into florets
- 3 russet potatoes, peeled and cut into equal size cubes
- 2 celery roots, peeled and cut into same size cubes as the potatoes
- 4 parsnips, peeled and cut into cubes
- 2 yellow onions, coarsely chopped
- 6 cups chicken stock
- 1 cup of cream
- A pinch of nutmeg
- Sea salt and freshly ground black pepper to taste

Sauté the onions in some butter and some salt in a pot until translucent. Add the vegetables and fill up with chicken stock until just covered. Cover the pot and simmer for about 20-25 min. until the vegetables are soft.

Let cool slightly, then add the nutmeg, salt, pepper and cream. Puree in batches in a blender. Place the soup in a clean pot to reheat, stir and taste for seasoning.

# South French Fish Soup

### Serves 4-6

- 1 ½ lbs. skinless cod, cut into 1 inch cubes
- 2 yellow onions, finely chopped
- 3 garlic cloves, chopped
- 2 tbsp. olive oil
- 1 fennel, cored and cut into thin strips
- 2 carrots, peeled and cut into thin sticks
- 4 firm potatoes, peeled and cut into small cubes
- 6 cups vegetable or fish stock
- 1 can of whole tomatoes
- ½ cup dry white wine
- A pinch of saffron
- Juice of 1 orange, or to taste
- Fresh basil or thyme to taste
- Sea salt and freshly ground black or white pepper

Gently sauté the onions and garlic in a big pot. After a few minutes, add the fennel, carrot and potatoes, thyme and stock. Cut the tomatoes with a pair of scissors and add to the pot with some salt and pepper.

Cover and let simmer for about 15 min. Add the wine and saffron and let simmer for another 10-15 min. until the vegetables are softened but somewhat firm. Add the fish and simmer until just done. Add the orange juice and herbs to taste and garnish with more herbs when serving.

# Curried Carrot and Apple Soup

### Serves 4-6

- 4 carrots, peeled and chopped
- 1 onion, coarsely chopped
- 1 celery rib, coarsely chopped
- 4 small apples, peeled, cored and coarsely chopped
- 1 tsp. curry
- 1 tsp. coriander
- 1 small piece of fresh ginger, grated
- Sea salt to taste
- 1 can of coconut milk
- Water A/N
- Canola oil A/N

Chop the vegetables and apples and sauté them gently in some canola oil. Add the spices and ginger when the vegetables are slightly softened and sauté a few minutes more. Add the coconut milk then water until the vegetables are just covered and let simmer for 20-30 min until the vegetables are very soft, but not mushy. Puree in a blender until smooth.

# Thai Chicken Soup

**Serves 4-6**

- 3 cups water
- 3 cups chicken stock
- ½ - 1 can coconut milk
- 1 tbsp. coconut oil
- 2 shallots, thinly sliced
- 2 tbsp. ginger, grated
- 4 lime leaves (optional)
- The bottom part of lemongrass, sliced lengthwise
- 2 chicken breasts, sliced into thin strips
- A handful of straw mushrooms (optional)
- Fish sauce to taste
- Lime juice to taste
- Whole cilantro leaves for garnish

Sauté the shallots gently in the coconut oil for a minute, then add the ginger, lemongrass and lime leaves. Lower the heat and cook very gently while stirring occasionally for a few minutes.

Add the water and chicken stock and simmer for 10 min. Add the chicken strips, mushrooms and coconut milk and simmer gently for another 5-10 min. Add fish sauce and lime juice to taste and season if necessary. Serve with the fresh cilantro leaves as garnish.

# Broccoli Soup

**Serves 6-8**

- 3 heads of broccoli
- 1 leek, sliced
- 1 onion, chopped
- 4 cups filtered water
- 3 potatoes, thinly sliced
- Vegetable stock, as needed
- 1 cup of cream
- Freshly ground white pepper and sea salt
- Fresh chives, chopped

Sauté the onion and the leek in a pan with the oil. Be careful not to brown the onions. Add the potatoes and broccoli and add vegetable stock until just covered. Simmer on low heat, covered, for about 30 minutes or until the potatoes are tender. Add the soup to a food processor in separate smaller batches to avoid getting soup on your kitchen wall.

Return everything to the pot. Add the cream (saving a little for serving), salt, pepper and heat up. Do not to overcook it at this point, as it will scorch or discolor. When serving, drizzle about a tablespoon of cream to each bowl, a few grinds of the white pepper and garnish with the fresh chives.

# Asparagus Soup

## Serves 6

- 1 bunch of asparagus
- 5 celery sticks, chopped
- 1 medium yellow onion, chopped
- 2-3 handfuls of red lentils
- 2-3 dollops of sour cream
- 3 cups filtered water
- 2 tsp. dried thyme
- 1 tsp. dried tarragon
- Sea salt and lemon pepper

Gently sauté the onion and celery for a few minutes in a deep pot, then add the asparagus, lentils and water. Let boil for 15-20 min. until the vegetables are soft but not mushy.

Let cool for a short while and then blend all ingredients in a food processor or with a hand mixer. Return the soup to the pot; add the chopped herbs, spices and sour cream and reheat. Serve with a small dollop of sour cream and a sprinkle of fresh herbs.

# Cold Melon and Cucumber Soup

## Serves 4-6

- 1 honeydew melon, peeled, seeded and chopped into cubes
- 4 Persian cucumbers, peeled and coarsely chopped
- 1 cup Greek yogurt
- Juice of 2 limes
- Pinch of cumin
- ½ bunch fresh mint
- ¼ tsp. salt
- ¼ tsp. freshly ground black pepper
- 4 tbsp. toasted sesame seeds

Combine all ingredients in a blender except the sesame seeds and run until smooth. Taste the soup and add lime juice, salt and pepper if desired.

Put into a covered bowl and refrigerate until cold, about 1 hour. Sprinkle with sesame seeds before serving.

# Pea Soup

**Serves 6**

- 2 cups of split peas
- 1 chopped yellow onion
- Knob of butter
- 3 cups organic chicken or beef stock
- ½ cup sliced ham
- 2 tsp. fresh marjoram or thyme
- 1 bay leaf
- 1 tbsp. Dijon mustard (when serving)
- Sea salt and freshly ground black pepper

Soak the peas in some water while chopping the onion. Sauté the onions in the butter until softened, then add peas, stock, ham and spices to the pot and simmer, stirring occasionally, for 40-60 min. until the peas are soft. If the soup is too thick in the end, just add more water. Add salt and pepper to taste and serve with 1 tbsp. of Dijon mustard.

# Arctic Avocado Soup

**Serves 4-6**

- 3 avocados
- 1 large leek, sliced
- 1 cup of crème fraiche
- 3 cups of cold vegetable stock
- Juice of 1 lemon
- Sea salt and freshly ground black pepper
- A pinch of chili powder (optional)
- Peeled and coarsely chopped English cucumber

Blend the avocado, leek and lemon juice with a mixer. Pour in the vegetable stock, crème fraiche and spices. Cover and keep in the fridge until cold. Serve over ice cubes, garnished with sliced cucumber.

# Sauces

## COLD SAUCES

# Roasted Pepper Sauce

- 3-4 red bell peppers
- 2 cloves garlic
- 1-2 cups mayonnaise
- Juice of half a lemon
- Pinch of ground chipotle
- Pinch of smoked or regular paprika
- Sea salt and freshly ground black pepper to taste

Roast the peppers by putting them directly over the fire on the stove. Turn with tongs until fully blackened on all sides. Place the peppers in a bowl and cover tightly with plastic wrap; let sit and 'steam' for 20-30 min. to loosen the skin. Peel the skin using a paper towel. Remove the seeds and pith, place in a food processor with the remaining ingredients and pulse until combined. Great as a condiment for crab cakes.

# Honey Mustard Sauce

- ½ cup white vinegar
- ½ cup honey or sugar
- 1- 1 ½ cup of mustard
- ½ - 1 cup canola oil
- ½ bunch fresh dill, chopped
- Sea salt and freshly ground black pepper to taste

Start by whisking the vinegar with the honey, salt and pepper until dissolved. Add the mustard, whisk, and then add the oil in a slow stream to emulsify. Add the dill and taste for salt and pepper.

# Cold Barbeque Sauce

- ½ cup crème fraiche
- ½ cup yogurt
- 1 tsp. BBQ seasoning
- 2 tsp. paprika
- 1-2 tsp. olive oil
- Pinch of garlic powder
- Sea salt and freshly ground black pepper

Mix all ingredients and let rest in the refrigerator for a while. This is great with grilled meats and veggies.

# Yogurt Tzatsiki

## Sauce

**Serves 6-8**

- 1 cup whole milk yogurt
- ½ cup chopped fresh dill
- 1 garlic clove, pressed (optional)
- ½ peeled, grated cucumber (optional)
- Juice of ½ - 1 lemon
- Sea salt and freshly ground black pepper

This is a great sauce to accompany fish, grilled meats or rice. Blend all ingredients; if you opt for the cucumber, after grating it, put it in a coffee filter or towel and squeeze to drain excess water before adding it to the mix. Chill for a while before serving.

# Cold Lemon Pepper Sauce

- ½ cup organic mayonnaise
- 2 tbsp. yogurt
- 2 tbsp. dried oregano
- A grind of lemon pepper
- ¼ cup water

Mix the ingredients in a small bowl; put the water in last to obtain the desired thickness. Grind the oregano between your fingers to enhance the flavor. Serve as a dip sauce for vegetables, salad dressing or as a side sauce for chicken. You can also add a pinch of curry powder for a different flavor.

# Spicy Sriracha Mayo

- ½ cup organic mayonnaise
- 1 tbsp. Sriracha sauce
- Pinch of ancho chili pepper
- Juice of half a lemon
- Salt and freshly ground black pepper to taste

Mix all ingredients in a bowl and taste for salt, pepper and lemon juice.

# Cold Barbeque Sauce

- ½ cup crème fraiche
- ½ cup yogurt
- 1 tsp. BBQ seasoning
- 2 tsp. paprika
- 1-2 tsp. olive oil
- Pinch of garlic powder
- Sea salt and freshly ground black pepper

Mix all ingredients and let rest in the refrigerator for a while. This is great with grilled meats and veggies.

## – HOT SAUCES –

# Tomato Sauce

- 1 large can organic chopped tomatoes
- 1 can tomato sauce
- 2-3 chopped tomatoes on the vine
- 3 chopped cloves of garlic
- 1 chopped medium onion
- 1-2 tbsp. dried oregano
- 1-2 tbsp. dried basil
- 1 tsp. dried thyme
- 1 tbsp. brown sugar (optional)
- 1 tsp. paprika
- 1 tbsp. soy sauce
- 2 tbsp. olive oil
- Sea salt and freshly ground black pepper

Begin by sautéing the onion in a pan with the oil; after a few minutes, add the garlic, lowering the heat slightly. Add the spices and stir continuously to allow the flavors to bloom. Crush the herbs with your fingers before sprinkling them into the pot.

After 30 seconds, pour in the soy sauce and add the chopped tomatoes. Add the fresh tomatoes and the other ingredients to the pot and let simmer for 1 hour. Add salt and pepper to taste.

---

# Chanterelle Sauce

- 1 lb. fresh chanterelles
- 2 tbsp. butter
- 2 shallots, minced
- 2 tbsp. flour
- ¼ cup white wine
- 1 cup chicken stock
- ½ cup cream
- Sea salt and freshly ground black pepper to taste

Clean the chanterelles thoroughly, using a brush to remove all dirt. Chop them coarsely and sauté on med-high heat with the butter. When browned, add the minced shallots to the pan and sauté a while longer while stirring occasionally. Add the flour and stir and cook for a minute. Add the wine followed by the chicken stock.

Reduce the stock and let it thicken for about 10 min. Whisk in the cream and reduce for another 5-10 min. Taste with salt and pepper and serve over your favorite meat.

# Béchamel

- 4 tbsp. butter
- 4 tbsp. wheat flour
- 1 cup of cream
- 1 cup of milk
- 1 bay leaf
- 4 cloves
- 1 garlic clove, thinly sliced
- Half an onion, sliced
- Sea salt and freshly ground black pepper

Make the sauce by melting the butter in a pot, being careful not to let it brown, then whisk in the flour and cook for a few minutes. Add the milk, cream, bay leaf, clove, onion, salt and pepper and heat slowly while whisking.

When you see the first bubble or small bubbles along the edge of the pot, reduce the heat and simmer while stirring with a spatula to scrape off any flour that may have attached to the edges. Simmer for 20-30 min. until all flour taste is gone, taste the sauce for salt and pepper and strain it. After straining, you can also flavor the sauce with your favorite herbs, Gruyère or cheddar cheese.

# Sauce Supreme

- 2 tbsp. butter
- 2 tbsp. flour
- 2-3 cups chicken stock
- ½ - 1 cups cream
- Juice of 1 lemon
- Sea salt and freshly ground black pepper to taste

Make the sauce by melting the butter in a pot, being careful not to let it brown, then whisk in the flour until it mixes and cook for a few minutes. Add the chicken stock and simmer for 10-15 min. until thickened and the flour taste is cooked off. Add the cream and simmer for another 5-10 min., then add the lemon juice and salt and pepper to taste.

# French Herb Sauce

- 2 tbsp. butter
- 2 tbsp. flour
- 2-3 cups chicken stock
- ½ - 1 cup cream
- Juice of half of a lemon
- 1 tsp. fresh tarragon, finely chopped
- 1 tsp. fresh parsley, finely chopped
- 1 tsp. fresh chives, finely chopped
- 1 tsp. fresh chervil, finely chopped
- Sea salt and freshly ground black pepper to taste

Make the sauce by melting the butter in a pot, being careful not to let it brown, then whisk in the flour until it mixes and cook for a few minutes. Add the chicken stock and simmer for 10-15 min. until thickened and the flour taste is cooked off. Add the cream and simmer for another 5-10 min, then add the herbs, lemon juice and salt and pepper to taste.

# Red Wine Reduction Sauce

- 1 tbsp. canola oil
- 2 shallots, minced
- ½ - 1 cup red wine
- 1 - 2 cups beef or veal stock
- 2 tbsp. cold butter
- Sea salt and freshly ground black pepper to taste

Sauté the minced shallots in the oil over medium heat in a sauce pan. Add the wine and deglaze the pan; let reduce until almost all the wine has evaporated. Add the stock and reduce until half of the liquid has evaporated. Cut the butter into chunks and mount the sauce by adding it piece by piece to the pan, swirling it at the same time. Taste the sauce and add salt and pepper to taste. A variation to this sauce is to add a few sprigs of fresh thyme after the onions have sautéed for a while.

# Pasta Sauce with Ham and Broccoli

**Serves 4**

- ¾ cup Black Forest ham, cut in ½ inch pieces
- 1 cup broccoli, cut in small bouquets
- 1 cup vegetable stock
- 4 tbsp. crème fraiche
- 3 tbsp. mayonnaise
- 3 cloves garlic, finely chopped
- 1 tbsp. paprika
- 1 tbsp. dried oregano
- Sea salt and freshly ground black pepper

This is a fast and delicious pasta sauce that almost makes itself! In a deep skillet, sauté the ham lightly in some olive oil; add the garlic after 3-4 min. then cook for another 2 min. Add the remaining ingredients and simmer for 10 min.

# Pasta Sauce with Red Pepper and Avocado

**Serves 4**

- ¾ cup of Black Forest ham, cut in ½ inch pieces
- 1 cup yellow onion, chopped
- 1 red pepper, sliced lengthwise
- ½ cup milk
- 4 tbsp. sour cream
- 3 cloves garlic, finely chopped
- ½ avocado, sliced in cubes
- Sea salt and freshly ground black pepper

In a deep skillet, lightly sauté the ham in some olive oil, add the onions and pepper and cook for about 2 min., until the onions and peppers are softened. Add the garlic and cook for another 2 min. Add the remaining ingredients except for the avocado and simmer for 10 min. When the sauce is ready, stir the avocado in gently and serve over pasta.

# Condiments

## — DIPS AND DRESSINGS —

# Avocado Butter

- 2 ripe avocados
- 2 tbsp. extra virgin olive oil
- Juice of 1 lemon
- Crushed chili pepper (optional)
- Sea salt and freshly ground black pepper

This is a great and delicious recipe to replace regular butter on sandwiches or as a party dip. Start by cutting the avocado in half and removing the pit. Cut the avocado length-wise in ¼ inch slices, then cut the slices into cubes. Put the avocado cubes into a mixing bowl. Add the remaining ingredients and whisk with a fork until desired smoothness is obtained.

# Guacamole

- 5 ripe avocados
- 1 red onion or 2 shallots, finely chopped
- 2-3 ripe tomatoes on the vine, cut into ¼ inch dice
- 1 bunch fresh cilantro
- 1 jalapeno, finely chopped (optional)
- Juice of 2 lemons
- Sea salt and freshly ground black pepper to taste

Start by cutting the avocado into cubes as explained in the above recipe. Mash the avocado cubes in a large mixing bowl along with the onions, tomato, salt and pepper. Lastly, add the lemon juice and fresh cilantro. Keep two pits to put in the dip, which helps the guacamole to stay fresh.

# Avocado Dressing

- 1 avocado
- ½ cup organic mayo
- ¼ cup of water
- 1 tbsp. mustard
- 1 tbsp. dried basil
- Sea salt and lemon pepper

For an avocado lover such as myself, there are never enough ways to prepare and use avocados. After cutting the avocado into cubes, put them in a food processor and blend in the remaining ingredients. Add the water last to achieve the desired thickness. Serve as a side sauce or over your favorite salad.

# Lime and Ginger Dipping Sauce

- 2 cloves garlic
- 2 tbsp. fresh ginger
- 2 cups mayonnaise
- Pinch of curry powder or turmeric
- ½ cup lime juice
- Sea salt and freshly ground black pepper to taste

In a food processor, chop the garlic and ginger. Add the rest of the ingredients and run until smooth. Taste for lime juice, salt and pepper; it should be taste light and fresh.

# Kalamata Olive and Caramelized Onion Spread

- 4 yellow onions
- 2 cups Kalamata olives, coarsely chopped
- 2 cups cherry tomatoes
- ½ cup olive oil
- 2 tsp. dried oregano
- Sea salt and freshly ground black pepper to taste

Start by roasting the tomatoes on a sheet pan at 350°F with some olive oil, salt and oregano for about 20 min until soft. Take them out of the oven and slice in quarters when cooled.

Slice the onions and caramelize in a pan with some butter, about 30 - 40 min. until deep brown, stir occasionally. Fold all ingredients in a bowl and taste for salt and pepper.

# Hummus

**Serves 6-8**

- 3 cloves garlic
- 2 tsp. ground cumin
- 2 tsp. ground coriander
- 1 tsp. paprika
- 2 cans of chickpeas/garbanzo beans
- ½ cup olive oil
- Juice of 2 lemons
- Sea salt and freshly ground black pepper to taste

Mince the garlic in a food processor. Add the other ingredients except for the olive oil. Run the processor and when well-combined, add the olive oil in a slow stream while running. Taste for all spices and lemon juice. Place in a bowl and add some paprika and olive oil on top.

# Spicy Chipotle Mayo

- ¾ cup mayonnaise
- 1-2 tbsp. sriracha chili sauce
- 1 tsp. lemon juice
- A pinch of ground chipotle powder
- Sea salt and freshly ground black pepper to taste

Combine all ingredients and serve wherever a spicy sauce is required.

# Roasted Pepper Dressing

- 2 tbsp. yogurt
- ½ cup mayonnaise
- ¼ cup finely diced roasted red peppers
- 1 tbsp. olive oil
- 2 tbsp. Water
- 3 tsp. paprika
- Sea salt and freshly ground black pepper

Mix all the ingredients in a food processor if available; otherwise, use a fork. Add the water last. Can be used as a dressing, dip or in a pasta salad.

# Baked Artichoke Dip

- 2 cans artichoke hearts, coarsely chopped
- 1 cup organic mayonnaise
- 1 cup grated Parmesan cheese
- 1 cup chopped green onions
- Sea salt and freshly ground black pepper to taste

Blend all ingredients in a bowl then place the mixture in a buttered glass baking dish and bake in the oven for 20 min. at 375°F. Serve as a dip with vegetables, corn chips or bread.

# – DRESSINGS –

## Ginger Salad Dressing

- 2 tbsp. grated fresh ginger
- 1 tbsp. white wine vinegar
- 4-5 tbsp. olive oil
- Juice of 1 lemon
- Dried herbs, thyme, rosemary, oregano
- Sea salt

Put the ginger, herbs, vinegar and lemon juice in a bowl. Stir vigorously with a balloon whisk and slowly add the olive oil until it emulsifies (thickens). Serve over salad.

## Mustard Dressing

- 6-8 tbsp. olive oil
- 2 tbsp. Dijon mustard
- 2 tbsp. white wine vinegar
- Juice of ½ of a lemon
- Sea salt and freshly ground black pepper

Blend the mustard, vinegar, salt, pepper and lemon juice in a bowl. Using a whisk, slowly add the olive oil until the dressing emulsifies. Serve as salad dressing or in a potato salad.

## Caesar Dressing

- 1-2 garlic cloves
- 3 anchovy fillets
- 2 tbsp. Dijon mustard
- Juice of 1 lemon, or more
- 1 tsp. dried oregano
- 1-2 cups organic mayonnaise
- ½ cup grated Parmesan
- Sea salt and freshly ground black pepper to taste

In a food processor, pulse the garlic until mashed. Add all ingredients except the Parmesan and run until combined. Add desired amount of Parmesan, pulse, and taste for salt and pepper.

## – MARINADES –

# The Meat Marinade

- 5 tbsp. olive oil
- 2 tbsp. soy sauce
- 2 cloves grated or pressed garlic
- ¼ cup red wine (optional)
- ½ cup chopped sun-dried tomatoes (optional)
- 2 tbsp. paprika

This is a fantastic marinade for steaks or pork tenderloin; although it is best if it can marinade in the refrigerator overnight, be sure the meat has time to sit in the marinade for at least an hour before cooking. Mix the ingredients, whisking the oil in last.

Smell the marinade to see if you think anything is 'missing,' then put the meat in and cover. If you are cooking the meat within an hour, allow it marinate at room temperature.

# The Poultry Marinade

- 5 tbsp. olive oil
- 1 tbsp. white wine vinegar
- ¼ cup white wine (optional)
- 2 cloves grated or pressed garlic
- 2 tbsp. lemon juice
- 2 tbsp. herbs de Provence
- Sea salt

This is a great marinade for chicken, turkey or white fish; although it is best if it can marinade in the refrigerator overnight, be sure the meat has time to sit in the marinade for at least an hour before cooking. Mix the ingredients, whisking the oil in last.

Smell the marinade to see if you think anything is 'missing,' then put the meat in and cover. If you are cooking the meat within an hour, allow it marinate at room temperature.

# Curry Marinade

- 5 tbsp. olive oil
- 2 tbsp. soy sauce
- 2 tbsp. lemon juice
- 2 tbsp. curry powder
- Sea salt

Put the ingredients in a bowl, pouring the oil last and whisking it in. Add salt to taste. This is great as a marinade for chicken or fish.

# Salads

# Assorted Field Greens with Shaved Red Onion in Raspberry Vinaigrette

**Serves 4-6**

- 2 cups baby romaine leaves
- 3 cups herb salad mix
- 1 cup wild arugula
- ½ red onion, sliced very thin
- 1 fennel
- 1 small can mandarin oranges in juice
- 3 tbsp. raspberry vinegar
- 1 tbsp. orange zest
- ½ tbsp. honey
- ¾ cup olive oil
- Sea salt and freshly ground black pepper

Shave the fennel using a mandolin or a sharp knife then submerge in ice water for 5-10 min. Combine the vinegar, orange zest and honey in a medium bowl. Whisk in the olive oil in a slow stream and season with salt and pepper.

Toss all ingredients in the dressing, being careful not to 'overdress' the salad, and serve immediately.

# Spinach Salad

## Serves 4

- 1 bag of spinach
- 1 cup strawberries, sliced
- ½ cup goat's cheese, crumbled
- 2 tbsp. balsamic vinegar
- A drizzle of olive oil
- Sea salt and freshly ground black pepper to taste

Combine all the ingredients in a salad bowl and drizzle the olive oil over them.

# My famous Coleslaw

## Serves 6-8

- 2 large carrots, grated
- 1 half head of green cabbage, sliced in strips
- ¼ head of red cabbage
- 2 shallots, minced
- 1 tbsp. Dijon mustard
- ½ cup mayonnaise
- ½ cup Greek yogurt
- 1-2 tbsp. apple cider vinegar
- 2 tbsp. dried oregano or fresh dill
- Juice of 1 lemon
- Sea salt and freshly ground black pepper

Grate the carrots and put them in a mixing bowl. A cheese slicer can be used to slice the cabbage; otherwise, just use a knife to slice thinly. Mix the cabbage with the carrots. Combine all other ingredients in a separate bowl, then toss well with the carrots and cabbage. Store it covered in the fridge.

# Arugula, Frisee and Apple Salad In Citrus Vinaigrette

**Serves 4-6**

- 2 cups arugula
- 2 cups frisee, the white part
- 2 green apples
- Juice of 1 lemon
- Olive oil A/N
- Sea salt and freshly ground black pepper

Start by peeling and coring the apples. Cut into small cubes and drizzle with lemon juice to prevent oxidization. Whisk remaining lemon juice with salt and pepper and add the olive oil in a slow stream. Toss all ingredients with the dressing and serve immediately.

# Spinach and Baby Arugula Salad with Champagne Vinaigrette

**Serves 4-6**

- 3 cups baby arugula
- 3 cups spinach
- 1 clove garlic, minced
- 1 shallot, finely chopped
- 2 tablespoons Dijon mustard
- ¼ cup champagne vinegar
- 2 tbsp. fresh lemon juice
- ½ tsp. salt
- ½ tsp. freshly ground black pepper
- ½ cup extra-virgin olive oil

In a bowl, mix together the garlic, mustard, vinegar, lemon juice, salt and freshly ground black pepper. Whisk in the olive oil in a slow continuous stream until the dressing has emulsified. Alternately, you can add the ingredients to food processor or blender and puree until smooth. Toss the dressing with the spinach and arugula and serve immediately. You can also use this dressing on any other salad.

# Fresh Herb Salad with Romaine, Carrots, Cherries, Walnuts and Blood Orange Vinaigrette

**Serves 4-6**

- 2 cups romaine lettuce
- 2 cups butter lettuce
- 2 cups carrots, peeled and cut into thin strips or diagonals
- 1 cup dried cherries
- ½ cup walnuts
- 4 tbsp. fresh blood orange juice
- 1 tbsp. lime juice
- 2 tbsp. white wine vinegar
- Olive oil A/N
- Sea salt and freshly ground black pepper

In a bowl, mix together the vinegar, juice, salt and black pepper. Whisk in the olive oil in a slow continuous stream until the dressing has combined. Toss all ingredients with the dressing and serve immediately.

# Asian Coleslaw

**Serves 6-8**

- 2 tbsp. rice vinegar
- ¼ tbsp. sugar
- 1 tbsp. fresh ginger, grated
- 1 tbsp. tamari or other soy sauce
- 4 tbsp. toasted sesame oil
- 2 green onions, chopped
- 1 ½ lbs. green cabbage, thinly sliced
- ½ lb. red cabbage, thinly sliced
- 3 celery ribs, thinly sliced
- 1 red bell pepper, thinly sliced

Combine the vinegar and sugar and whisk to dissolve. Add ginger, green onions and soy sauce and blend. Whisk and add the sesame oil in a slow stream to make a temporary emulsion. Toss the salad with the dressing; cover and chill for 30-60 min. Toss the salad again before serving.

# Cucumber and Cocktail Tomato Salad with Fresh Herbs

### Serves 4-6

- 6 Persian cucumbers
- 2-3 cups cocktail or cherry tomatoes
- ½ cup fresh dill, chopped
- ¼ cup fresh parsley, chopped
- Sea salt and freshly ground black pepper
- Juice of 1 lemon
- Olive oil A/N

Cut the cucumber once lengthwise then cut into fairly thin half-moons. Quarter the tomatoes. Whisk the lemon juice with salt and pepper and add the olive oil in a slow stream. Toss all ingredients with the dressing and serve immediately.

# Leafy Green Salad with Cranberry and Gorgonzola

### Serves 4

- 1 bag mixed leafy baby greens
- 1 tomato, chopped
- ½ cup Gorgonzola, crumbled
- ½ cup cranberries
- ½ cup walnuts, coarsely chopped
- Drizzle of olive oil
- Sea salt and freshly ground black pepper

Soak the walnuts in some water and sea salt for at least 10 min., then pat dry or roast before chopping; this makes them juicier and easier to digest. Chop the nuts and mix them with the remaining ingredients in a bowl. Top with olive oil, some sea salt and freshly ground black pepper.

# 3 Bean Salad

### Serves 6-8

- Juice of 2-3 lemons
- ½ - 1 cup olive oil
- 2 shallots, finely chopped
- 1 tsp. cumin
- 1 bunch fresh cilantro, finely chopped
- Sea salt and freshly ground black pepper to taste
- 2 cans kidney beans
- 2 cans pinto beans
- 2 cans garbanzo beans

Combine the lemon juice, shallot, cumin, cilantro, salt and pepper then whisk in the olive oil in a slow stream to emulsify. Toss the dressing with the beans and let rest for a short time at room temperature.

# Garden Fennel Salad

## Serves 4

- 1 bag mixed baby greens
- ½ bag arugula
- 1 fennel, sliced
- 1 large carrot, grated
- ½ large yellow pepper, chopped

Dressing:
- 4 tbsp. olive oil
- 2 tbsp. apple cider vinegar
- 1 tsp. Dijon mustard
- Sea salt and freshly ground black pepper

Make the dressing by mixing the salt and pepper with the mustard and vinegar, then pour in the oil slowly while whisking until the dressing thickens. Toss all the vegetables in a mixing bowl with the dressing.

# Sesame Asparagus Salad

## Serves 4-6

- 2 bunches of asparagus, ends removed and sliced in 1 inch diagonals
- 1 tbsp. honey
- 2 garlic cloves, minced
- 2 tbsp. soy sauce
- 3 tbsp. sesame oil
- 2 tbsp. sesame seeds

Blanch the asparagus in salted boiling water for a few minutes, making sure they remain firm. Transfer to an ice bath to stop cooking, strain and dry. Combine the honey, garlic and soy sauce. Whisk in the sesame oil in a slow stream. Toss the asparagus with the dressing and sesame seeds and serve.

# Classic Salad

### Serves 4-6

- 6 cups romaine lettuce, sliced 1 inch thick
- 3 tomatoes, halved and sliced
- ½ English cucumber, sliced
- 1 red bell pepper, sliced

Dressing
3 tbsp. olive oil
Sea salt and pepper
Juice of ½ lemon

Combine the vegetables in a salad bowl and drizzle with the oil, followed by the lemon juice, salt and pepper. You can also use one of the dressings from the index.

Including a starch in a main meal is important to achieve balance in its ratio. There are plenty of theories as to what constitutes the healthiest and most balanced ratio of protein, carbohydrates and fat. These diet hypes are often contradictory and insist that everything from low fat, low carbohydrate, zoning, counting calories, etc. is your single best diet solution. The truth of the matter is, one always needs to try to achieve a healthy balance when making food choices. What are most important to consider are the quality of the food and the quantity that is consumed at any given time; for instance, if you consume excessive carbohydrates in one sitting, the extra energy will get stored in your body as fat.

The same thing is true if you eat too small a portion of carbohydrates, which will leave you feeling lethargic and unsatisfied. To help digest the protein and fat in a meal, an appropriate amount of carbohydrates is essential. Finding the amount that is right for you is what is important., and the best way to do that is to start with a small amount in proportion and increase gradually, testing your way to a balanced meal proportion. If you feel like falling asleep within 1-3 hours after eating, chances are you had too much carbohydrate. The same thing is true if you get sweet cravings shortly after your meal, in which case you probably had too much protein and fat relative to carbohydrates.

Below are some easy and highly nutritious recipes you can create for a balanced sustained energy source that you can always rely on. A good idea is to make a larger quantity of whatever you are cooking to have a batch that last all week. Most of the recipes can easily be doubled if you need larger quantities.

# Corn and Bean Salad

## Serves 4

- 1 cup corn, cooked
- 1 cup black beans, cooked
- 2 tomatoes, chopped
- 1 cup cucumber, chopped
- 1 shallot, finely chopped
- ½ bunch cilantro, chopped
- Juice of ½ lemon
- 3 tbsp. olive oil
- Sea salt and freshly ground black pepper

Mix the corn and black beans. Chop the tomatoes, cucumber and shallot and add to the beans. Fold in the chopped cilantro and add the rest of the ingredients.

# Sides

## – VEGETABLES –

Adding vegetables to your meal will not only make it taste better but will actually help you digest your food and assimilate all the nutrients in it. Always try to have at least one type of vegetable with every meal so you get your daily intake of vitamins, minerals and trace elements.

# Sautéed Spinach

### Serves 2-4

- 1 bag spinach
- 3 cloves garlic, chopped
- 3 tbsp. olive oil
- A pinch of nutmeg (optional)
- Herbamare herbal salt (see sources)

Sauté the garlic on low heat in the olive oil or butter if preferred, add the spinach and fold until softened. Be careful not to overcook as it will get mushy and release a lot of liquid. Sprinkle herbal salt and freshly ground black pepper over the spinach and serve immediately.

# Chard

### Serves 4-6

- 1 bunch green chard
- 2 cloves garlic, chopped
- ½ cup sour cream
- Juice of 1 lime
- Herbamare herbal salt

Sauté the chard until soft, then add the garlic and sauté a while longer. Stir in the sour cream and lime juice. Finish with a sprinkle of herbal salt.

# Roasted Sweet Potato with Pine Nuts

### Serves 4-6

- 4-5 sweet potatoes, peeled and cut into ½ inch cubes
- 2 shallots, finely chopped
- 2 garlic cloves, minced
- ½ cup pine nuts
- 4 thyme sprigs
- ¼ cup Parmesan cheese
- Olive oil A/N
- Sea salt and freshly ground black pepper to taste

Preheat the oven to 400°F. In a large mixing bowl, toss all ingredients except the Parmesan and place in a single layer on a large baking sheet. Roast for 25-30 min., turning once halfway.

After 20 min. or so, sprinkle the Parmesan over and finish cooking for 10 min. Serve immediately.

# Mustard Turmeric Roasted Cauliflower

**Serves 4-6**

- 1 head cauliflower, cut into florets
- 2 tbsp. Dijon mustard
- 1 tsp. fresh lemon juice
- ½ tsp. turmeric
- 1 garlic clove, minced
- 1 tsp. sea salt
- ½ tsp. freshly ground black pepper
- ¼ cup olive oil, or A/N
- A pinch of saffron
- A pinch of red chili flakes

Preheat the oven to 425°F. Combine all ingredients except the cauliflower and olive oil in a mixing bowl. Whisk in the oil in a slow stream until emulsified.

Toss the cauliflower in the dressing and spread evenly in one layer on a baking sheet. Roast for about 20 min., turning once halfway. It's ready when somewhat soft and just starting to blacken on the top.

# Creamed Mustard Greens with Parmesan

**Serves 4-6**

- 1 bunch mustard greens
- 1 tsp. Dijon mustard
- 4 tbsp. cream
- ½ cup Parmesan
- Sea salt and freshly ground black pepper

Slice the mustard greens into ½ inch strips and sauté them in a skillet with some olive oil. When soft, stir in the mustard and cream followed by the Parmesan. After the mustard and cream integrates, add salt and pepper to taste.

---

# Steamed Vegetables

**Serves 4-6**

- 1 fennel
- 1 large carrot
- 1 onion
- ½ yellow pepper
- 3 cloves garlic, sliced coarse
- 2 tbsp. herbs de Provence
- Sea salt and olive oil

This is a great way to make delicious and nutritious vegetables as a side dish. Cut all the vegetables into rather large wedges and place in a steamer.

Drizzle the oil and then the spices over the vegetables and steam for about 5-7 min., until firm but tender. Add a drizzle of olive oil if desired. Serve immediately.

# Zucchini Boats with Mango Vegetable Relish

### Serves 6-8

- 4 zucchini, cut lengthwise with the center scooped out, leaving a 1/8 inch rim
- Olive oil A/N
- Sea salt and freshly ground black pepper
- 2 ripe mangos, peeled and cut into ¼ inch cubes
- 1 red bell pepper, pith removed and cut into ¼ inch dice
- 2 Persian cucumbers, peeled and cut into ¼ inch cubes
- Juice of 1 lemon
- 1 jalapeno, seeded and finely chopped
- 2 tbsp. fresh cilantro, finely chopped

Preheat the oven to 350°F. Drizzle olive oil and sprinkle with salt and pepper on both sides of the zucchini.

Place cut side down on a baking sheet and bake for about 10-15 min. until the zucchini is fork tender but not mushy. Combine all ingredients for the relish in a mixing bowl and let macerate for 20 min. Turn the zucchini over and fill the scooped out cavity with the relish. Serve at room temperature.

# Green beans with Shiitake Mushroom and Bacon

### Serves 4-6

- 1 lb. green beans, ends trimmed
- ½ lb. shiitake mushroom
- 5 strips bacon, chopped
- 2 garlic cloves, minced
- Sea salt and freshly ground black pepper to taste

Soak the mushrooms in water for 5-10 min. Remove from the water, squeeze out the excess and chop into thin strips. Fill a large pot with water and salt and let come to a rapid boil. Blanch the green beans for 5-7 min., until tender but firm.

Transfer to an ice bath to stop cooking. Strain when cold and let dry. In a large skillet, brown the bacon over medium heat with some oil. When crispy, remove the bacon from the pan and increase the heat.

When the bacon fat shimmers, add the mushrooms and sauté over high heat until browned. Reduce the heat and add the garlic while tossing the contents of the pan.

After a minute, add the dried beans to the pan and reheat while stirring occasionally. When hot, return the bacon to the pan, toss, and serve immediately.

# Zucchini Stir-Fry

**Serves 4-6**

- 2 green zucchini
- 1 eggplant
- Canola oil, as needed
- 2 tomatoes, chopped
- 4 tbsp. sesame seeds
- 2-3 tbsp. garam masala
- 1 tbsp. garlic powder
- 3 tsp. sea salt

Sauté the eggplant first on high heat with some canola oil then remove from pan and repeat with the zucchini. When done, add the zucchini to the eggplant. Sauté the tomatoes for about 3 min., add the other vegetables back, toss and add the garam masala and sesame seeds. Serve hot.

Start by preparing the eggplant, slicing it lengthwise and lengthwise again, and then cut the strips in half. Marinade them in some olive oil and garlic powder. Cut the zucchini diagonally into equal sized strips.

# Broccoli and Cheese

**Serves 6-8**

- 4-6 cups broccoli, cut into florets
- 2 eggs
- 1 cup cottage cheese
- ¾ cup cheddar cheese, shredded
- 1 bunch green onions, chopped
- ½ cup ham, diced (optional)
- Sea salt and freshly ground black pepper

Preheat the oven to 375°F. Steam the broccoli for 3-4 min. They should be quite firm. If you don't have a steamer, you can fill the bottom of a pot with water.

Put in the broccoli and cover with a lid. Halfway through, stir so that the broccoli in the bottom does not get overcooked. Put the broccoli in a square or rectangular buttered baking dish with edges so the broccoli covers the bottom. Blend the remaining ingredients in a mixing bowl and pour over the broccoli. Bake in the middle of the oven for 20-25 min. until golden brown.

# Fennel and Cauliflower Gratin with Black Summer Truffle Sauce

### Serves 6-8

- 4 fennel bulbs, cut into thin wedges
- 1 head cauliflower, cut into florets
- 1 batch béchamel sauce (See index.)
- 1 fresh black summer truffle, slivered, or good quality truffle oil
- Panko bread crumbs A/N
- Knobs of butter

Make the béchamel sauce, adding the truffles in the beginning. When the sauce is done, let it rest covered with a plastic film for 30 min. for the flavors to come together before straining.

Fill a large pot with water and salt and bring to a rapid boil. Blanch the vegetables in batches until tender but firm.

Transfer to an ice bath to stop cooking. Strain when cold and let dry. Place the vegetables in a large mixing bowl and season with a little salt and pepper. Toss to coat the vegetables in the sauce and place evenly in a ceramic casserole. Sprinkle bread crumbs on top and place knobs of butter over. Bake in the oven at 350°F 20-25 min. until browned. Let rest slightly before serving.

# Beet Salad with Cracked Coriander and Pistachio

**Serves 4-6**

- 6 medium beets, stems removed
- 1 tbsp. lemon juice, plus zest cut in strips
- 4-6 tbsp. pistachio oil
- 2 tbsp. toasted and cracked coriander seeds
- Sea salt and freshly ground black pepper
- Micro basil for garnish, optional

Place the beets in lightly salted water and cook covered until tender, 35-45 min. Mix the lemon juice, coriander seeds, salt and pepper in a bowl. Whisk in the oil in a slow stream. Check for seasoning. When the beets are done, rinse in cold water until cool enough to handle.

Peel the skin off gently and cut each beet into 6-8 wedges. Fold the beets with the dressing and let macerate for at least an hour or overnight. Garnish with the micro basil and some more coriander seeds and lemon zest.

# Sautéed Okra in Tomato Sauce

## Serves 6-8

- 1 ½ lbs. fresh okra
- 1 red onion, finely chopped
- 3 garlic cloves, minced
- 1 6 oz. can of tomato paste
- Chicken stock A/N
- 1 tbsp. ground cumin
- 2 tsp. dried oregano
- 4 tbsp. olive oil
- Sea salt and freshly ground black pepper to taste

Heat the olive oil in a large skillet until shimmering, then add the onions and sauté with a pinch of salt until softened. Add the garlic and spices and cook for 2 min. while stirring. Add the okra and continue to cook until they start to brown. Add the tomato paste, stir and cook for another 2 min. Add chicken stock while stirring gently until a sauce forms. Simmer for 10-15 min until the okra is soft but not mushy. Check for seasoning and serve.

# Roasted Asparagus with Peas And Basil

## Serves 4-6

- 2 bunches asparagus, woody ends removed, cut into 1 inch pieces on a diagonal
- 3 cups frozen peas, thawed
- 1-2 shallots, finely chopped
- 2 tbsp. butter
- ½ cup fresh basil, cut into fine strips
- Sea salt and freshly ground black pepper to taste

Sauté the shallots over medium heat in a deep skillet with some sea salt, stirring occasionally until softened. Add the asparagus and peas, cover and cook for about 6-8 min. The asparagus should still be crisp. Sprinkle the basil over, stir, check for seasoning and serve.

# Curry Wok

### Serves 4-6

- 2 heads bok choi, sliced
- 1 head broccoli, cut into small bouquets
- 1 red pepper, sliced in strips
- 1 fennel, sliced
- ½ onions, chopped
- 4 cloves garlic, chopped
- 1 cup roasted tofu
- ¾ cup peanuts
- 3 tbsp. tamari
- 2 tbsp. curry powder
- 2 tbsp. olive oil
- 2 tbsp. coconut oil
- Sea salt to taste

In a large wok, heat the oils and sauté the onions, peppers and fennel for a few minutes. Add the broccoli, bok choi and garlic and sauté for a few minutes more. Add the curry and tamari followed by a quick stir. Lastly, fold in the tofu and peanuts and add salt to taste.

# Grilled Asparagus

**Serves 4**

1 bunch fresh asparagus

For the marinade:
- 3 tbsp. olive oil
- 2 cloves garlic, chopped
- Juice of ½ lemon
- Sea salt and freshly ground black pepper
- Chili seeds (optional)

After cutting off and disposing of the woody ends of the asparagus, blanch them in salted boiling water for 2 min.

Take out the asparagus and place them in an ice bath to stop the cooking, then grill them on high heat in a grill pan or on a grill until slightly charred.

Mix all the ingredients for the marinade and add the asparagus. Let soak for at least 5-10 min. Alternately, you can pre-marinade them, grill them and simply put them back in the marinade.

# Cauliflower Puree

**Serves 4-6**

- 1 head cauliflower, cut into equal size florets
- 3-4 tbsp. butter
- 3 tbsp. cream
- 2 tsp. sea salt
- Pinch of nutmeg (optional)

Place the cauliflower in a pot, cover with water, and season with salt. Bring to a boil and simmer covered for 7-8 min. until softened. Avoid either over- or undercooking as the cauliflower will either release too much liquid or be too chunky. Add the butter and seasoning and mash or pulse in a blender. Add the cream last to obtain the right consistency. Note: The cauliflower can easily be replaced with peeled and cut carrots; just adjust the cooking time accordingly.

# Mixed Vegetable Casserole with Israeli Couscous

**Serves 6-8**

- 2-3 cups Israeli couscous
- 2 sweet potatoes, peeled and cut into ½ inch cubes
- 3 zucchini, washed, ends removed and cut lengthwise twice then into ½ inch cubes
- ½ head cauliflower, cut into florets
- 8 cups chicken stock
- 1 cinnamon stick
- A pinch of saffron
- A pinch of ground cinnamon
- Sea salt
- 4 tbsp. butter
- 2 tbsp. fresh parsley

In a big pot, let the chicken stock come to a boil with the saffron, cinnamon stick and some sea salt. Blanch the vegetables in batches until soft but somewhat firm, remove using a strainer and set aside in a colander. Keep the liquid and let come to a boil between batches. After all the vegetables are blanched, add the couscous and half of the butter. Cook while stirring occasionally until done. Strain the couscous but keep some of the liquid. Toss all ingredients with the remaining butter and the cinnamon and parsley. Check for seasoning and serve hot.

# Beet Salad with Balsamic Dressing

### Serves 4-6

- 6 medium beets, stems removed
- 2 tbsp. good quality balsamic vinegar
- 1 small shallot, minced
- ½ tbsp. Dijon mustard
- 1 tbsp. lemon juice
- 4-6 tbsp. olive oil
- A pinch of dried oregano
- Sea salt and freshly ground black pepper

Place the beets in lightly salted water and cook covered until tender, 35-45 min. Mix the shallots, vinegar, mustard, oregano and salt and pepper in a bowl. Whisk in the oil in a slow stream. Check for seasoning. When the beets are done, rinse in cold water until cool enough to handle. Peel the skin off gently and cut each beet into 6-8 wedges. Fold the beets with the dressing and let macerate for at least an hour or overnight. NOTE: you can also use this dressing for your favorite salad.

# Rosemary and Honey-Roasted Parsnip and Celery Root

### Serves 4-6

- 4 medium-sized parsnips, peeled and cut into ¼ inch cubes
- 2 celery roots, peeled and cut into ¼ inch cubes
- 3 carrots, peeled and sliced diagonally into 1/8 inch pieces
- 1-2 tbsp. rosemary, chopped
- ¼ cup plus 3 tbsp. olive oil
- 1 shallot, minced
- 1 ½ tbsp. white balsamic vinegar (optional)
- 1 tbsp. honey
- Sea salt and freshly ground black pepper

Preheat the oven to 400°F. Place the vegetables on a baking sheet and drizzle with the 3 tbsp. of olive oil, add the rosemary, salt and pepper and toss well. Arrange in an even layer and roast for about 35 min. until golden brown, turning over once. Mix the remaining olive oil in a bowl with the rest of the ingredients and toss with the vegetables. Let cool slightly and serve.

# Grand Marnier Braised Fennel

**Serves 4-6**

- 5 large fennel, rinsed and cut into 6-8 wedges, including the root
- 4 tbsp. olive oil
- ½ cup Grand Marnier
- ½ cup orange juice
- Sea salt and freshly ground black pepper

Heat a thick-bottomed skillet, add the olive oil and wait until shimmering. Alternately, you can use a combination of canola and olive oil. Place the fennel with the cut side down first and sear until well-browned. Check each individual piece as you go along and turn over to the other side. When turned, season with salt and pepper. As soon as both sides are well-browned, pour in the Grand Marnier and cover quickly. Let cook for a few minutes, remove the lid and let the remaining liquid reduce to almost dry. Pour in the orange juice, cover again and turn the heat to low.

The fennel are ready in about 10-15 min., when they are very soft and tender. At this point, remove the lid and reduce the liquid further for a greater depth of flavor. Check the seasoning and serve hot.

# Butternut Squash and Lentil Tagine

### Serves 4-6

- 1 whole butternut squash, 1-1 ½ lbs.
- 2 tomatoes
- ¼ cup olive oil
- 1 onion, finely chopped
- 3 garlic cloves, minced
- 1 tbsp. tomato paste
- 1 ½ cups brown lentils
- ½ tsp. ground cumin
- ½ tsp. turmeric
- 1 tsp. paprika
- Chicken stock A/N
- Fresh parsley, chopped
- Sea salt and freshly ground black pepper to taste

Rinse the lentils, put in a pot and add chicken stock just to cover. Let simmer for 20-25 min. until softened, adding more stock if necessary. Halve the tomatoes, remove the seeds and chop finely. Peel and seed the squash and cut into 1 inch cubes. Heat a large deep skillet and add the oil. When shimmering, sauté the onions with a pinch of salt for a few minutes. Add the garlic and sauté for a minute longer.

Add the spices and cook until aromatic, then add the tomato paste. Stir for 30 sec. before adding the tomatoes and squash. Toss well, add a little chicken stock, cover and cook for 10 min. When the squash is halfway done, add the lentils to the pot. Add more chicken stock if dry, cover again and cook until the squash is soft and the flavors have merged. Check for seasoning and sprinkle the parsley on top when serving.

# Sautéed Radishes with Orange Juice

### Serves 4-6

- 2 lbs. radishes cut into quarters with some stem attached
- 3 tbsp. unsalted butter
- 3 large shallots, thinly sliced
- 1 tbsp. sugar
- 1 cup fresh orange juice
- Salt and freshly ground black pepper

Melt the butter in a large skillet and add the shallots. Sauté the shallots gently until softened and add the radishes. Cover and cook over moderately high heat, stirring occasionally, until browned. Add the sugar and stir until dissolved; add the orange juice. Cook until the radishes are tender, season with salt and pepper and serve.

# Eggplant
## Parmesan

### Serves 6-8

- 2 large eggplants
- 2 batches tomato sauce (See index.)
- 1 cup Parmesan cheese
- 3 tbsp. olive oil
- 3 tsp. garlic powder
- Sea salt and freshly ground black pepper

Preheat the oven to 375°F. Peel the eggplant and slice in 1/8 inch slices. Put them aside in a bowl with a little olive oil, garlic powder and sea salt.

When making the tomato sauce, use tomato paste instead of tomato sauce as this will make the sauce thicker. Grill or sauté the eggplant. Cover the bottom of the dish with sauce, followed by the eggplant, then a sprinkle of Parmesan. Continue to layer the eggplant with the tomato sauce and Parmesan until all of the eggplant and sauce is used.

Bake in the oven for 35-40 min. Pierce the center with a fork to see if the eggplant is soft.

# Sweet and Sour Braised Endives

### Serves 4-6

- 1 lb. Belgian endives
- 2-3 tbsp. honey
- 3 tbsp. fresh lemon juice or white wine vinegar
- ½ cup chicken broth
- Olive oil A/N
- Sea salt and fresh freshly ground black pepper

Remove the outer leaf of the endive and cut lengthwise. Drizzle olive oil to coat both sides and season with salt and pepper.

Whisk together the honey and lemon juice. Heat some oil in a deep, lidded skillet until the oil is shimmering. Sear the cut side first until browned, then turn to brown the other side. Lower the heat, turn the endives back over and add the honey/lemon mixture, shake the skillet to coat. Add the chicken broth and cover. Simmer for 5-10 min. until the endives are fork tender. Check the seasoning and serve.

# Beet and Avocado Salad

### Serves 4-6

- 3 cups beets, about 2-3 bunches
- 1 clove garlic, chopped
- 3 stems green onion, chopped
- ½ cup parsley, chopped
- 2 ripe avocados, cut into ¼ inch cubes
- Olive oil A/N
- Sea salt and freshly ground black pepper to taste

Steam or boil the beets until softened but still firm, about 30-45 min. Plunge into an ice bath to stop cooking. Cut them into 1/3 inch thick slices or wedges. Add the remaining ingredients except for the avocado and fold together with a spatula. Lastly, add the avocado, fold gently and check for seasoning. Let flavors merge a few minutes in the refrigerator before serving.

# Caramelized Brussels Sprouts

## Serves 4-6

- 1 lb. Brussels sprouts
- 5 slices bacon or pancetta, cut into 1/8 inch dices
- Canola oil A/N
- Sea salt and freshly ground black pepper to taste

Cut the root of the Brussels sprouts and cut once lengthwise. Blanch the Brussels sprouts in boiling salted water until soft but still firm, about 10 min. Plunge into an ice bath, strain and pat dry with a paper towel.

In a thick-bottomed skillet, render the bacon using a little oil and a splash of water over medium heat. When crisp, remove the bacon from the pan, keeping the fat in the skillet. Turn the heat on high and add more oil if necessary. When the pan is hot, place the Brussels sprouts cut side down to brown. Turn over to brown the other side and season with salt and pepper.

# Zucchini and Bok Choi Gratin

## Serves 6-8

- 4-5 large zucchini,
- 5 bok choi
- ¼ cup olive oil
- 2 shallots, finely chopped
- 1 garlic clove, minced
- 1-2 tbsp. dried thyme
- ½ cup grated Parmesan
- ½ cup panko breadcrumbs
- Sea salt and freshly ground black pepper

Preheat the oven to 350°F. Cut the ends of the zucchini, cut lengthwise twice, followed by cutting into equal ½ inch cubes. Cut off the root end of the bok choi, then, separating the stem from the leaves, cut the stem and root sections into equal size pieces.

Blanch the vegetables in batches in boiling salted water until soft but not mushy, then place into ice bath. Strain and dry the vegetables and mix them in a bowl.

Sauté the shallots in the olive oil over medium heat with some salt; after a few minutes, add the garlic and thyme. When aromatic, pour the oil mixture over the vegetables and toss. Season with salt and pepper if desired.

Place the vegetables in an oven proof casserole in an even layer and sprinkle with the combined Parmesan and breadcrumbs. Dot with butter or olive oil and bake for 20-25 min. until the crust is somewhat golden.

# Roasted Green Beans, Cauliflower and Fingerling Potatoes

## Serves 6-8

- 1 lb. fingerling potatoes, scrubbed but not peeled
- 3 cups cauliflower, cut into equal size florets
- 1 lb. green beans, ends trimmed
- 4 garlic cloves, finely chopped
- 1 tsp. smoked paprika
- 2 tbsp. sherry vinegar
- Olive oil A/N
- Sea salt to taste

In a large pot, cover the fingerling potatoes with water, add salt and bring to a boil. Simmer until almost tender, about 8 min. Add the green beans and cauliflower and simmer for another 5 min. until all vegetables are soft but firm. Meanwhile, sauté the garlic gently with the olive oil over low heat until fragrant. Strain the vegetables and put in a mixing bowl. Add the olive oil, garlic, sherry vinegar and smoked paprika. Toss well and serve immediately.

# Whole Grains

# Basic Brown Rice

### Serves 4-6

- 4 cups filtered water or chicken stock
- 2 cups brown rice
- 2 tbsp. olive oil
- 2 tsp. sea salt

Heat up a medium-sized pot and put in the rice to 'roast' it gently. Have the water ready and, stirring occasionally, test the rice with your fingertips to make sure it does not get too hot. Pour the water in just before the rice starts to burn your fingers. Add the oil and salt. Cover and let come to a boil.

Put the heat on the lowest setting and let simmer for 40 min. Take the lid off, fluff the rice lightly with a fork and let sit for another 5-10 min. before serving. Note: Optional spices and vegetables can easily be added to your basic rice to give it more character or to accompany a certain dish. For example, add dried basil, oregano or thyme after you put in the water, oil and salt. You can also switch to brown wild rice and add roasted almond slivers before serving.

# Brown Rice with Lentils

### Serves 4-6

- 2 cups brown rice
- 5 cups filtered water
- 1 cup red lentils
- 2 tbsp. olive oil
- Sea salt and herbs de Provence

Follow the above recipe; just rinse the lentils and add them with the rice.

# Green Rice with Parsley

### Serves 4-6

- 2 cups brown rice
- 4 cups filtered water
- 1 cup frozen organic sweet peas
- 1 cup chopped fresh parsley
- 2 tbsp. olive oil
- Sea salt

Use the recipe for basic brown rice but after 35 min., add the peas and parsley, make a quick stir and allow it to sit with no heat for 10-15 min. Taste the rice to be sure that it is fully cooked. If you do not have brown rice, you can replace it with white, basmati or jasmine rice; in that case, reduce the cooking time to 15-20 min before adding the other ingredients.

# Pasta Salad

**Serves 6-8**

- 3 cups whole wheat penne or fusili
- 3 tomatoes, chopped
- ½ cup sun-dried tomatoes, soaked and then chopped
- 2-3 shallots, chopped
- 1 cup Kalamata olives, sliced
- 1 cup cucumber, chopped (optional)
- 1 cup red bell peppers, chopped (optional)
- 3 tbsp. dried mixed herbs
- Sea salt and pepper

Cook the pasta in a large pot filled with water, some olive oil and salt, then drain and rinse with cold water.

Chop all ingredients while the pasta is cooking and mix everything in a big bowl.

From this point, you have a lot of choices; either simply dress it with avocado oil or olive oil or use one of your favorite dressings from above. You can also add chicken, turkey, ham, shrimp or any other kind of meat you like.

# Saffron Orzo Salad, Cherry Tomatoes, Green Onions, Parsley, Mint and Lemon Juice

**Serves 4-6**

- 2 cups orzo (rice-looking pasta)
- A pinch of saffron
- ¼ cup olive oil or A/N
- 4 green onions, finely chopped
- 4 cups chicken or vegetable stock
- 1 cup cherry tomatoes, quartered
- ½ cup fresh parsley, finely chopped
- ¼ cup fresh mint finely chopped
- Juice of 1 lemon
- A pinch of sea salt

Cook the orzo in the stock with the saffron as directed on the packet. Strain and add olive oil and let cool. Prepare the rest of the ingredients and toss it all together, add salt and pepper to taste and let rest at room temperature for a while to let the flavors combine. This is an excellent summer side dish.

# Avocado Rice

**Serves 4-6**

- 2 cups brown rice
- 2 cups water
- 2 cups coconut milk
- 1-2 diced avocados
- Lemon pepper
- Sea salt

Add the rice and water to a pot and let come to a boil. Reduce the heat and simmer for 20 min. Add the coconut milk, stir once, and simmer for another 20 min. Gently stir in the chopped avocado, lemon pepper and salt. Let sit for a minute before serving. An optional squeeze of lemon can be added if desired.

# Quinoa

**Serves 4-6**

- 2 cups quinoa
- 4 cups filtered water
- 1 vegetable stock cube
- 2 tbsp. olive oil
- 2 tsp. sea salt

Quinoa is a fantastic grain with a high protein content that has a full and balanced spectrum of amino acids, making it the only grain with complete amino acid content. If you have time, the quinoa benefits from being soaked overnight.

If not, soaking for 10 min. or so will do, as this will reduce a bitter flavor that the quinoa can have otherwise. Place the quinoa, water, olive oil, stock cube and the salt in a pot. Bring to a boil, then reduce the heat and let simmer for 15-20 min. Turn off the heat when the water is almost absorbed, allowing the quinoa to swell a little before serving.

# Black Rice Salad with Mango

**Serves 4-6**

- 2 cups black (often referred to as forbidden) rice
- 4 cups filtered water
- 2 chopped tomatoes
- 1 cup chopped fresh basil
- ½ cup chopped dried or fresh mango (optional)
- 2 tbsp. olive oil
- Sea salt

Forbidden rice is great for you as it is high in fiber, minerals and amino acids. As in vegetables, more color suggests a higher density of nutrition.

Put the rice, water, oil and salt in a medium stainless steel pot, cover and let come to a boil. Reduce the heat to low and simmer for 40-50 min. Stir in the tomatoes, mango and basil and let sit for 10 min. Taste the rice to see if more salt or oil is needed.

# Red Quinoa

### Serves 4-6

- 2 cups red quinoa
- 4 cups filtered water
- 1 vegetable stock cube
- 1 leek, sliced
- 1 red pepper, sliced
- 1 large carrot, grated
- 2 cups green peas
- Juice of 1 lemon
- 2 tbsp. olive oil
- 3 tbsp. ghee (clarified butter)
- 2 tsp. herbal salt or sea salt

In a pot, start by sautéing the carrot and leek in the olive oil until soft. Place the quinoa, water, stock cube in the pot and let come to a boil. Reduce the heat and let simmer for 15-20 min.

Turn off the heat when the water is almost absorbed. Meanwhile, sauté the red pepper in half of the butter on low heat. When soft, add the lemon juice, herbal salt and let the peppers sit in the juice until the quinoa is done.

Fold in the peppers, peas and add the rest of the butter. Wait for a few minutes before serving.

# Quinoa with Broccoli and Peppers

**Serves 4-6**

- 2 cups quinoa
- 4 cups filtered water
- 1 vegetable stock cube
- 2 crowns broccoli, cut in small florets
- 1 yellow onion, chopped
- 1 green pepper, sliced
- 1 bunch fresh cilantro, chopped
- 4 tbsp. olive oil
- Juice of 1 lemon
- 2 tsp. sea salt

Place the quinoa, water, half of the olive oil, the stock cube and the salt in a pot and let come to a boil; reduce the heat and let simmer for 10-15 min. Add the broccoli and let simmer for another 5 min. Turn off the heat, keeping pot covered. Meanwhile, sauté the peppers and onions gently in the rest of the oil and put aside. Blend the peppers and onions into the quinoa after it is cooked and add the lemon juice and cilantro. Serve immediately.

# Cardamom and Star Anise Jasmine Rice Pilaf

**Serves 4-6**

- 2 cups jasmine rice
- 4 cups filtered water
- 1 onion, finely chopped
- 3 tbsp. olive oil
- 1 tbsp. butter
- ¼ cup cardamom pods
- ¼ cup star anise
- 4 cloves
- 1 cinnamon stick
- 2 tsp. sea salt

Put the oil and butter in a medium pot; heat slightly before adding the onions. Sauté until very soft and translucent and add the cardamom, star anise, cloves and cinnamon. While stirring, cook until fragrant. Add the rice and keep stirring for a minute. Add the water and salt, cover, and let simmer for 20 min. on low heat. Let sit for a few minutes, fluff with a fork and serve.

# Mediterranean Couscous

**Serves 4-6**

- 2 cups of whole grain couscous
- 1 ¾ cups of water
- 1 small red onion, chopped
- 1 ½ cups cherry tomato sliced in quarters
- 1 red pepper sliced in strips
- 1 bunch fresh basil, chopped
- 4 tbsp. olive oil
- Sea salt and pepper

Boil the water and add the oil and salt. Pour in the couscous, turn off the heat, cover and let sit for 5 min. Meanwhile, sauté the onions and peppers. (They can also be added raw.) Mix all ingredients together, saving some fresh whole basil leaves for an attractive and flavorful garnish.

# Orzo with Pistachio

**Serves 4-6**

- 2 cups orzo
- 1 small onion, finely chopped
- 4 cups vegetable stock
- 1 cup pistachio nuts, chopped
- 1-2 tbsp. cardamom, ground
- 1 tsp. cloves, ground
- ½ bunch fresh basil, chopped
- A pinch of sea salt

Cook the orzo in the stock as directed on the packet, strain and put back in the pot. In a separate pot, sauté the onions in some oil for a few minutes then add the spices. Let the flavors merge for a minute, then add the nuts and basil. Mix all with the orzo and serve immediately.

# Bulgur with Sausage

**Serves 4-6**

- 2 cups bulgur or cracked wheat
- 4 cups vegetable stock
- 1-2 leeks, sliced
- 1 cup crumbled feta cheese
- 1 cup spicy chorizo, sliced
- ¼ cup fresh parsley, chopped (optional)
- Sea salt and pepper

Sauté the sausage for a few minutes, then add the leeks to the pan. Add the bulgur and the stock and cook for about 30-40 min. Add salt and pepper to taste.

# Saffron Rice

### Serves 4-6

- 2 cups basmati rice
- 4 cups filtered water
- 1 chopped onion
- 3 tbsp. olive oil
- 1 tbsp. butter
- ½ gram crushed saffron strands
- 2 tsp. sea salt

Put the oil and butter in a medium pot, heat slightly before adding the onions. Sauté until translucent, then add the saffron. Stir to 'bloom' the flavor until the onions turn yellow.

Add the rice and keep stirring for a few minutes. Add the water and salt and let simmer covered for 20 min. on low heat. Let sit for a few minutes, fluff with a fork and serve. Note: If you do not have saffron, substitute 2 tsp. turmeric and 2 tsp. of curry powder for a different style of deliciously colorful rice.

# Cracked Wheat with Herbs

## Serves 4-6

- 2 cups cracked wheat
- 4 cups vegetable stock
- 2 tomatoes, finely chopped
- 1 cup red cabbage, shredded
- ½ cup fresh parsley, chopped
- ½ cup fresh cilantro, chopped
- ½ cup fresh basil, chopped
- Juice of 1-2 limes
- 2 tsp. sea salt

Cook the cracked wheat and cabbage in the stock for about 40 min. Fold in the tomatoes and herbs towards the end. Squeeze in the lime juice, then add some olive oil.

# Vegetable Lasagna

## Serves 6-8

- ½ packet of whole grain lasagna sheets
- 3 zucchinis, sliced diagonally
- 2 eggplants
- 1-2 batches basic tomato sauce (See index.)
- ½ cup mozzarella cheese
- ½ cup Parmesan cheese

Preheat the oven to 375°F. Peel the eggplant and slice into 1/8 inch slices. Put them aside in a strainer after sprinkling each side with sea salt. Leave for 30 min. until you see excess water being expelled, then rinse the eggplant briefly and pat dry. Create the basic tomato sauce. Slice the zucchini and grill or panfry them and the eggplant separately. Layer all of the ingredients in a large baking dish, starting with some of the tomato sauce and adding the pasta sheets and sautéed eggplant, followed by a little more tomato sauce. Lastly, add the zucchini and put a thin layer of tomato sauce on top. Blend the cheeses and sprinkle over the lasagna. Bake in the oven for 30-40 min. until the cheese turns golden. Let it rest a little before serving.

# Buckwheat Noodles with Spinach

**Serves 4**

- 1 pack buckwheat noodles
- 1 onion
- 3 garlic cloves
- 1 bag spinach

Chorizo option:
- 2 sliced chorizo sausage
- 2 chopped tomatoes
- 2 tsp. ground paprika
- Sea salt and pepper

Seafood option:
- 1 cup shrimp or crab meat
- ½ squeeze lemon
- ½ small can capers
- Fresh ginger, grated

Cook the noodles with the sea salt and olive oil, strain and rinse with cold water to prevent sticking. In the meantime, brown the sausage first; when browned, add the onions and lastly, the garlic and spices.

After a few minutes, when you smell the aroma of the onions and the garlic, add the spinach and tomato. Add the cooked and strained noodles to the pan and splash with soy sauce. For the seafood option, use shrimp or crab instead of sausage and add the ginger with the garlic. Add lemon juice and capers in the final step.

# Protein Noodles with Shrimp and Garbanzos

**Serves 4**

- 1 packet protein enhanced noodles
- 1 can garbanzo beans
- 1/2 to 1 lb. shrimp, peeled
- 4 cloves garlic
- 1/2 sliced red onion
- 1 cup chopped Kalamata olives
- 4-5 tbsp. hummus (optional)
- Sea salt and freshly ground black pepper

Cook the protein noodles with olive oil and sea salt. In a large skillet, sauté onions, shrimp and garlic until they are golden. Add spices and fold in the hummus, garbanzos and olives. Add the noodles to the pot and serve with a squeeze of lemon.

# Soba noodles
## with Green Onions and Plum Vinegar

**Serves 4-6**

- 1 packet soba noodles
- 4 green onions, chopped
- 2-3 tbsp. toasted sesame oil
- 1-2 tbsp. plum vinegar
- 1 tbsp. tamari or other soy sauce
- 2 tbsp. sesame seeds

Cook the noodles as directed on the packet with a pinch of salt. Strain and rinse immediately to prevent them from sticking together. When ready to serve, heat the oil in a skillet on low heat and add the noodles and green onion. When the noodles are hot, add the rest of the ingredients, toss the pan and serve right away.

# Quinoa with Dried Fruits and Almonds

### Serves 4-6

- 2 cups quinoa
- 4 cups filtered water
- 2 tbsp. olive oil
- 1 tbsp. turmeric
- 2 tsp. paprika
- 1 tsp. ground ginger
- ½ cup raisins or currants
- ½ cup slivered almonds
- 2 tsp. sea salt

Place the quinoa, water, olive oil, raisins and the spices in a pot and let come to a boil; reduce the heat and let simmer for 15-20 min. Turn off the heat, add the almonds and let sit for a few minutes before serving.

# Millet with Vegetables

### Serves 4-6

- 2 cups millet
- 4 cups filtered water
- 1 large fennel, thinly sliced
- 3 celery sticks, chopped
- 1 squash, sliced
- 1 jalapeno, sliced (optional)
- 2 tbsp. dried mixed herbs with lavender (optional)
- 2 tbsp. olive oil
- 2 tsp. sea salt

Sauté the vegetables in the oil for a few minutes, add the millet, water, salt and simmer for about 20 min. until all liquid is absorbed. Fold in the herbs and top off with some more olive oil.

# Potatoes

# Boiled Potatoes

## Serves 6-8

- 6-8 whole potatoes, russet, golden or red
- 3 tbsp. butter, melted
- Water, filtered
- 2 tsp. sea salt

If the potatoes are large, cut into quarters. I prefer to leave the skin and retain all of the vitamins and minerals that it contains. Put the potatoes in a pot with the salt and add water until it just about covers the potatoes. Bring to a boil, then turn the heat down and simmer for about 20 min. Test the potatoes with a fork to see if they are soft. An optional bay leaf can be added to the pot for a different flavor. Drain, toss with the butter and serve.

# Duchesse Potatoes

## Serves 6-8

- 6-8 russet potatoes
- 4 oz. (1 stick) butter
- 2 oz. cream, or as needed
- 4 oz. grated Parmesan cheese
- 2 egg yolks
- Sea salt and ground white pepper to taste

Preheat the oven to 350°F. Follow the recipe for mashed potatoes but add the Parmesan and egg yolks when folding everything together. In a ceramic casserole, use a piping bag or simply spoon the potatoes in an even layer. Bake the potatoes in the oven for 20-25 min. until slightly browned on top.

# Potato Gratin

### Serves 6-8

- 20 medium golden potatoes, peeled and sliced into 1/8 inch slices
- 1-2 yellow onion, halved and sliced
- 1 cup cream
- 1 cup milk
- 1 bay leaf
- 4 cloves
- ½ onion, sliced
- 2 cups of 'aged' cheese, grated
- 3 tbsp. wheat flour
- 4 tbsp. butter
- Sea salt and pepper

Preheat the oven to 400°F. Make a béchamel sauce by melting the butter in a pot, being careful not to brown it, then whisk in the flour until it mixes and cook for a few minutes. Add the milk, cream, bay leaf, clove, onion, salt and pepper and heat slowly while whisking.

When you see the first bubble or small bubbles along the edge of the pot, lower the heat and simmer while stirring for 20 min. Taste the sauce and strain it. In a large buttered baking dish, preferably ceramic or glass, layer the sliced potatoes, not too tight to allow the sauce to disperse through the layers, followed by a layer of sliced onion.

Add some pepper from the mill and a sprinkle of salt then repeat the process until the baking dish is filled. Pour the sauce over the potatoes and place the dish in the oven.

After 25 min., take the dish out and if the level of fluid is lower than half of the pan, add some cream; otherwise, just add the cheese evenly and put it back in the oven for another 20-25 min. until the cheese is golden brown. Take out and let rest for 10-15 min. before serving.

# My Mashed Potatoes

### Serves 6-8

- 6-8 russet potatoes
- 4 oz. (1 stick) butter
- 2 oz. cream, or as needed
- Sea salt and ground white pepper to taste

Peel the potatoes and put them in some water to rinse and prevent oxidization. Cut them into equal size cubes, lengthwise then lengthwise again and then into 2-3 pieces, depending on size of the potatoes.

Put the potatoes in a pot and use just enough cold water to cover; add a generous amount of salt. Cover and let come to a simmer. Test the potatoes frequently and strain when just fork tender. Meanwhile, melt the butter in a separate pot and add the cream.

When the potatoes are dry, pass them preferably through a food mill or potato press for creamy and fluffy mashed potatoes. Add salt and pepper and fold to incorporate the cream; if too dry, add more cream. Taste for salt and pepper and serve hot. If you don't serve immediately, reheat gently over low heat while folding.

# Roasted Garlic Mashed Potatoes

**Serves 6-8**

- Serves 6-8
- 6-8 russet potatoes
- 4 oz. (1 stick) butter
- 6 garlic cloves
- Olive oil A/N
- Sea salt and ground white pepper to taste

Follow the above recipe for mashed potatoes but before cooking the potatoes, add the garlic cloves to a small pot and cover with olive oil. Simmer the garlic on low heat until very soft, about 30-45 min. Puree the garlic and add to the mash in the folding stage.

# Mashed Potatoes with Bacon, Crème Fraiche and Chives

**Serves 6-8**

- 6-8 russet potatoes
- 4 oz. (1 stick) butter
- 2 oz. crème fraiche, or as needed
- Half a pack of bacon, about 5 slices
- 20 sprigs of chives, finely chopped
- Sea salt and ground white pepper to taste

Cook the bacon in the oven at 350°F for 10-15 min. until crisp but not too hard, place on a paper towel and reserve the drippings to add to the mash if desired. Chop the bacon into fairly small pieces. Follow the recipe for mashed potatoes and fold all ingredients together.

# Potato Salad

## Serves 10-12

- 30-40 small golden potatoes or 20-30 red potatoes
- 1 cup cherry tomatoes, halved
- 1 cup garbanzo beans, strained
- 1 cup Kalamata or green olives, sliced
- ½ cup sun-dried tomatoes, chopped
- ½ cup capers
- 1 batch mustard dressing (See index) or simply sherry vinegar and olive oil

OR

- 30-40 small golden potatoes or 20-30 red potatoes
- 1 ½ cup mayonnaise
- ½ cup water
- ½ cup capers
- ¼ cup shallots, finely chopped
- 1 bunch dill, chopped
- Juice of 1 lemon
- Sea salt and pepper

Cut the potatoes in ½ inch cubes and boil in water with sea salt for 5-10 min. until just tender. Make sure not to overcook, as you want them firm. When cooked, strain and array the potatoes on a large baking tray and allow to air dry and cool.

Meanwhile, chop the remaining ingredients and make the dressing. When the potatoes have cooled, first add the tomatoes, beans, capers and olives and then mix in the dressing. Finish with some sea salt and a few turns of the pepper mill. If you like, sprinkle some Italian herbs over as well.

For the second option, blend the mayonnaise and water with the rest of the ingredients and fold it in with the potatoes. Make sure the potatoes are cold or they will 'melt' the dressing. Let marinade for a while before serving. It can also be served at room temperature or refrigerated for later use.

# Oven Roasted Potatoes with Root Vegetables

**Serves 6-8**

- 5 large russet or golden potatoes
- 3 large carrots
- 3 fresh beets
- 2 parsnips
- ½ cup feta cheese (optional)
- ½ cup fresh thyme
- 4 tbsp. olive oil
- 2 tbsp. sea salt

Preheat the oven to 400°F. Cut the potatoes and vegetables in relatively large wedges, e.g., for the potatoes, cut them in half and cut the halves in 2-4 wedges.

Add the vegetables and potatoes to a big baking dish and drizzle the oil over them. Add the thyme and sea salt and toss to coat. Bake in the middle of the oven for about 40 min. until golden brown.

After 20 min., turn the vegetables over once with a flat spatula to redistribute the oil and to allow even cooking. Let cool slightly before serving. If you opt for the feta cheese, add it to the dish after 35 min.

# Oven Roasted Peppers and Sweet Potatoes

**Serves 6-8**

- 4 sweet potatoes
- 1 red pepper
- 1 green pepper
- 1 red onion
- 1 yellow onion
- 4 garlic cloves, chopped
- 4 tbsp. olive oil
- 2 tbsp. sea salt

Preheat the oven to 400°F. Peel and cut the sweet potatoes in ½ inch thick slices, the onions in 6 wedges each and the peppers in large rectangular pieces, also removing the white pith.

Add the vegetables and potatoes to a large baking dish and drizzle the oil over it. Add the sea salt and toss. Bake in the middle of the oven for about 40 min. until golden brown. After 20 min., turn the vegetables with a flat spatula. Let cool slightly before serving.

# Mashed Sweet Potatoes

**Serves 6-8**

- 2 large russet potatoes
- 3 large sweet potatoes
- 1 cup of milk, or cream
- ½ cup of chicken or vegetable stock (optional)
- 6-10 tbsp. butter
- ¾ cup parsley or ¾ cup sage, chopped (optional)
- 3 tsp. sea salt and freshly ground black pepper

Peel the sweet potatoes but not the regular potatoes; just wash the skin and cut into cubes slightly smaller than the sweet potatoes. Cut the sweet potatoes in ½ inch cubes and put both potatoes in a big pot of filtered water. Simmer covered for 20-25 min. Pierce a piece with a fork to check that they are thoroughly but not overcooked, as that may make them gummy when mixed. Strain and let the water evaporate. Melt the butter in a separate pot and add the milk or cream and the herbs (optional). Preferably, pass the potatoes through a food mill or potato press so that they don't get overworked; that can also make the mash gummy. Add the butter and milk or cream and fold the mixture gently; add more milk or butter and optional stock if the mash is too firm. Add sea salt and black or white pepper to taste. The same recipe can be used with only regular potatoes for classic mashed potatoes; just replace the sweet potatoes with the same amount of russet potatoes.

# Beans and Lentils

Beans and Lentils are greatly unappreciated and often forgotten side dishes to accompany your meal. Served classically on brown rice, or to give a protein dish an extra dimension, they are also highly nutritious and add protein as well as fiber to your meal. Below are a few simple ways to make delicious beans and lentils. You can use dry beans if you want; just let them soak overnight or precook them slowly for 4-5 hours. Most of us do not have that extra time so organic canned beans work great and are easy to use.

# Cashew and Pineapple Lentils

**Serves 4-6**

- 1 cup red lentils
- 1 cup green lentils
- 1 large carrot, grated
- 1 medium onion, chopped
- 1 cup cashews, coarsely chopped
- 1 cup fresh pineapple, chopped
- 1 vegetable stock cube
- 2 tbsp. curry powder
- 2-3 cups water, filtered
- A pinch of sea salt

Gently sauté the onion and carrot in some olive oil in a pot; after 3-5 min., add the curry. Allow the flavors to bloom for a minute, then add the lentils and cook for another 3 min. Add the water, salt and stock cube. Simmer on low heat for 20 min. Towards the end, when the lentils are getting soft and most of the water is absorbed, add the cashews and pineapple. Turn off the heat and let rest for 5 min. before serving.

# Cinnamon Lentils

**Serves 4-6**

- 1 cup red lentils
- 1 cup green lentils
- 1 large carrot, grated
- 1 cup almonds, coarsely chopped (optional)
- 1 cup fresh coconut, shredded
- 2 tbsp. cinnamon
- 2-3 cups water, filtered water
- A pinch of sea salt

Gently sauté the carrot in olive oil in a pot; after 3-5 min., add the cinnamon and the lentils and cook for another 3 min. Add water and salt. Let simmer on low heat for 20 min. Towards the end, when the lentils are getting soft and most of the water is absorbed, add the almonds and coconut. Turn off the heat and let rest for 5 min. before serving.

# Classic Pinto Beans

### Serves 4

- 1 can pinto beans
- 1-2 shallots, chopped
- 1 spicy sausage or ham, chopped (optional)
- ½ cup filtered water
- 1 vegetable stock cube
- Paprika
- Sea salt and freshly ground black pepper

Begin by sautéing the shallots in some olive oil for a few minutes; add the chopped sausage or ham to brown.

Make creative use of whatever you have in the fridge.

Add the spices, and wait a minute before adding water and stock cube. Take half of the beans and mash them on a plate with a fork or with a hand blender before putting it in the pot. Add the beans and simmer for 10-15 min. Be careful not to overcook beans as they will lose flavor and turn into mush.

---

# Black Beans a' la Puerto Rico

### Serves 4-6

- 2 cans black beans
- 4 garlic cloves, chopped
- ½ yellow onion, chopped
- 1 bay leaf
- ½ cup chicken stock
- ½ cup filtered water
- 1 small can of tomato sauce
- Sea salt and pepper
- If you want to spice it up a little, add your favorite herbs or red pepper flakes in the end.

Sauté the onions in some olive oil for a few minutes then add the garlic and sauté gently. Mash half of one can of the beans with a fork and add it to the pot with the remaining ingredients. Simmer for 15-20 min. Add salt and pepper to taste and serve.

# Red Beans

- 3 cans red beans (pinto beans can also be used)
- ½ cup olive oil
- 4 garlic cloves, chopped
- 1 onion, finely chopped
- 1 bunch cilantro, finely chopped
- Sea salt and freshly ground black pepper to taste

In a medium pot, heat the oil with the garlic, onions and cilantro. After the onions have browned slightly, add the beans to the pot and simmer for 5-10 min. Add salt and pepper to taste and serve.

# Garbanzos in Herbs

**Serves 4**

- 1 can garbanzos
- 1 yellow onion, chopped
- ½ cup filtered water
- Fresh parsley, chopped (can be switched to rosemary)

This is probably one of the easiest recipes for beans and it is delicious. Sauté the onions until translucent, then add the beans with the liquid from the can, water and parsley (or rosemary), allow to simmer for a few minutes and it is done.

# The Quiche

A quiche is a great side dish that everybody appreciates; it is a perfect complement to a festive occasion and a great addition to the table as a side dish. It is quite easy to do but takes a little more time because the dough needs to rest for a while, it requires some additional time in the oven as well as resting when done. There are almost endless variations as to what you can add to your quiche or pie, limited only by your imagination. A few examples follow the base dough recipe. The recipes can easily be doubled if you want to make two quiches. Another option is to omit the dough, making a frittata to slice up and serve as an appetizer.

# The Base Dough

- 2 cups flour (you can use half whole grain or spelt)
- 1 ¾ sticks butter (200 g)
- 1 egg
- 1 tbsp. cold water
- 2 tsp. sea salt

Slice the butter into small cubes and add to the flour; mix with fingers until the butter is pea-sized. Add the egg, water, salt and quickly work into dough. Form a disc, wrap it in plastic wrap and refrigerate to rest for 30-40 min.

---

# Portobello and Spinach Quiche

### Serves 6-8

- 1 batch base dough
- 1 bag fresh spinach
- 4 large Portobello mushrooms
- 3 garlic cloves, chopped
- 1 cup walnuts, chopped and soaked
- 4 whole eggs and 1 egg yolk
- 2 cups cream
- 1½ cups milk
- Sea salt and freshly ground black pepper

Preheat the oven to 400°F. Use a dowel to flatten the dough to fit a buttered 12-inch round pie pan. Make sure the dough attaches a little over the edge of the pan and crinkle the edges with a fork or fingers. Place a piece of plastic wrap over the crust and fill it with uncooked beans, then wrap the plastic wrap over. Bake for 7-10 min.; take the pie crust out of the oven and remove the beans and plastic wrap. Bake for an additional 7-10 min., being careful not to over-brown the crust.

Soak the mushrooms in water for a few minutes, then squeeze the water out of them with your hand as you would with a sponge. Slice the mushrooms into ¼ inch strips and sauté with butter for a few minutes at a fairly high temperature.

When you note that the mushrooms are getting soft, add the spinach and chopped garlic to the pan and turn off the heat, adding the salt and pepper. Fold once or twice to wilt the spinach. Add the mushrooms and spinach to the piecrust and top off with the walnuts. In a mixing bowl, whisk the eggs, milk, and cream and add some salt and pepper. Pour the batter into the pie pan and bake in the oven for 30-40 min. until golden brown, checking with a tester stick in the center to make sure it is cooked through. Let rest a little before serving.

# Salmon and Goat's Cheese Quiche

### Serves 6-8

- 1 batch base dough
- 1 cup smoked salmon, chopped
- ½ - 1 cup goat's cheese, crumbled
- 1 leek, sliced and sautéed
- 4 whole eggs and 1 egg yolk
- 2 cups cream
- 1½ cups milk
- Sea salt and freshly ground black pepper

Spread the salmon, leek and goat's cheese evenly over the pre-baked crust (see recipe above). Add the egg batter and bake in the oven for 30-40 min. until golden brown. Let rest slightly before serving.

# Chanterelle Quiche

### Serves 6-8

- 1 batch base dough
- 2 cups fresh chanterelle, chopped
- 1 onion, chopped
- 1 cup chives, chopped
- 1 cup crème fraiche
- 4 eggs
- 1 cup cheese, strong (i.e., aged cheddar)
- Sea salt and freshly ground black pepper

If you do not have access to fresh chanterelles, dried will do; just soak them in water for a while before chopping them. Brown off the onions and mushrooms in some butter and put in the pre-baked pie shell. Blend the eggs, crème fraiche, cheese and chives in a mixing bowl with some salt and pepper. Pour the batter into the pre-baked crust and bake in the oven for about 30-40 min. until golden brown. Let rest a little before serving. Garnish the pie with the remainder of the chives.

# Cheese Quiche

**Serves 6-8**

- 1 batch base dough
- 1 onion, chopped
- 2 cups cheese, strong
- 4 whole eggs and 1 egg yolk
- 2 cups cream
- 1½ cups milk
- Sea salt and freshly ground black pepper
- A pinch of nutmeg
- 1 cup fresh dill, chopped (optional)

Preheat the oven to 400°F. Sauté the onion and put it into the pre-baked piecrust. Blend the eggs, milk, cream and cheese. Add the spices, pour the batter into the piecrust and bake in the oven for 30-40 min. until golden brown. Let cool for a short while. Garnish with the dill before serving.

# Roasted Butternut Squash and Caramelized Onion Quiche

**Serves 6-8**

- 1 batch base dough
- 3 onions, sliced
- 1 medium-sized butternut squash
- 1 cup grated Parmesan
- 4 whole eggs and 1 egg yolk
- 2 cups cream
- 1½ cups milk
- Sea salt and pepper

Preheat the oven to 400°F. Cut the peeled butternut squash into ½ inch cubes, toss with olive oil and sea salt and spread evenly in one layer on a baking sheet. Roast for 15 min., turn over once with a spatula and roast for another 15 min or until soft.

Meanwhile, sauté the onions on low heat with some butter, turning frequently until deep brown and caramelized, about 30-40 min. Mix the squash and onions and put it into the pre-baked piecrust, followed by a sprinkle of Parmesan. Blend the eggs, milk, and cream, pour the batter into the piecrust and bake for 30-40 min. until golden brown. Let rest for a short while.

# Meats

There have almost always been strong opinions, with many stating that meat is bad for you, which is interesting since it has been a staple food (almost exclusively in some cultures) since well before modern civilization. Quality meat provides the most essential proteins and is very important to maintaining a healthy balance of the diet. Whenever someone asks me why Swedish people tend to be tall and beautiful, I reply: "because we eat foods of great quality consisting of a lot of meat, potatoes and vegetables." The meats are the power food on your plate; be sure to choose the highest quality, do not overcook it and you can enjoy meat free of guilt. It is also a good idea to rotate your meat sources for variety and nutrition.

# Meatloaf

**Serves 6-8**

- 2 lbs. ground beef
- 2 large carrots, grated
- 1 large yellow onion
- ½ cup milk
- 1 cup breadcrumbs
- 4 whole eggs, lightly whisked
- Sea salt and white pepper

Preheat the oven to 375°F. Soak the breadcrumbs with the milk for 5 min. Grate ½ of the onion and 1 carrot manually with a grater, or in a food processor. Add it along with the spices and let sit for another 3 min. Blend in the ground meat with your hands and add the eggs. Be careful not to overwork the mix, as the meat will turn stringy.

Place into a buttered medium sized baking dish with edges and shape it into an even rectangular shaped loaf. Slice the remaining onion and carrot and put them on the sides of the meat loaf. Alternately, olive oil can be drizzled over the vegetables. Bake in the oven for 40-50 min. Check the internal temp with a thermometer; the meat loaf should be at about 155°F when ready. Remove from oven and let rest covered for 10-15 min. before serving.

# Beef Burgers with Thyme and Garlic

**Serves 4-6**

- 1 lb. lean ground beef
- ½ cup oats or bread crumbs
- ¼ cup cream
- 4-5 cloves garlic, minced
- 3 tbsp. butter
- 2 whole eggs, lightly whisked
- 2-3 tbsp. dried thyme
- 2 tsp. sea salt
- freshly ground black pepper

Start by soaking the oats with the cream for 5 min., then add the minced garlic and thyme. Let sit for another 3 min., blend in the ground meat with your hands and add the eggs. Let the flavors combine for 10 min. at room temperature before shaping patties with your hands.

Heat a large skillet, add the butter and wait until the pan is very hot and the butter is nut colored. Place the patties in the pan and brown for a few minutes on each side until thoroughly cooked. Alternately, they can be cooked in the oven for 20-30 min. at 450°F, but they will not have the same nicely browned appearance.

# Whole Roasted Pork Tenderloin with Freshly Ground Black Pepper Crust

## Serves 4-6

- 1 whole pork tenderloin, silverskin removed
- 1 bay leaf
- 1 tsp. ground mustard
- 2 tbsp. freshly ground black pepper, coarsely ground or A/N
- 2 tbsp. sea salt or A/N
- Canola oil for frying
- Kitchen string

Preheat the oven to 350°F. Grind the bay leaf in a spice grinder to a fine powder and combine with the other spices. Tie kitchen string around the tenderloin with 1 inch spacing.

Roll the whole piece of tenderloin in the spice blend to fully cover the surface. Heat a thick-bottomed skillet; when very hot, pour the oil in, wait for 30 sec. and sear all sides of the tenderloin until nicely browned.

Transfer to a baking sheet and roast in the oven for about 20 min. Check the internal temp at the thickest part and pull it out when the temperature reads 155°F. Cover with foil and let rest for 10-15 min. to finish cooking, then slice.

# Grilled Filet Mignon

### Serves 4

- 4 two inch pieces filet mignon, rinsed and dried
- 1 batch meat marinade (See index.)

Preheat the oven to 375°F. Make the marinade and let the meat absorb the flavors for at least an hour at room temperature. It is best if it can marinate in the fridge overnight; just take it out half an hour before to make sure it is at room temperature before cooking.

Heat a grill, grill pan or regular pan until it is very hot, then place the pieces in the pan to brown off the surface for about 2 min. on each side. If you use a grill, turn the pieces 90 degrees after a minute or so to make a nice grill pattern. Place the pieces in a baking dish and put them in the oven until they are cooked to your preference. 3-5 min. for rare, 5-7 min. for medium and 10-12 min. for well done.

# Grilled Skirt Steak in Sesame Cilantro Marinade

**Serves 4-6**

- 1 ½ lbs. skirt steak, trimmed of excess fat
- 3 tbsp. tamari or soy sauce
- 2 tbsp. rice vinegar
- 2 cloves garlic, minced
- 1 tbsp. fresh ginger, grated
- 2 green onions, finely chopped
- ½ cup fresh cilantro, finely chopped
- 2 tbsp. toasted sesame seeds
- 5 tbsp. toasted sesame oil
- 2 tbsp. canola oil

Take each trimmed piece of skirt steak and place between 2 pieces of plastic wrap. Pound the steak into ¼ inch even thickness with a mallet.

Make the marinade by combining all ingredients except the oils in a mixing bowl, then add the oils in a slow steam while whisking. Taste and check for seasoning and oil to acid balance.

Submerge the skirt steak into the marinade and let sit for 1-24 hours. Heat a grill and sear both sides for nice grill marks and flavor; reduce the heat and cook until desired doneness is obtained. Let rest for a few minutes, slice against the grain and serve. If no grill is available, slice the pieces against the grain before putting it in the marinade and stir fry on high heat with some canola oil.

# Braised Short Ribs

### Serves 6-8

- 3 lbs. beef short ribs bone in, cut into 2x2 inch squares
- 2-3 tbsp. ground coriander
- 2 onions, coarsely chopped
- 3 carrots, peeled and coarsely chopped
- 4 garlic cloves, coarsely chopped
- 1 14 oz. can San Marzano chopped tomatoes
- 1 ½ cups red wine
- 4 thyme sprigs, whole
- 1 bay leaf
- 4 cups beef stock
- 1 tbsp. balsamic vinegar
- 2 tbsp. fresh parsley, finely chopped
- Sea salt and freshly ground black pepper
- A blend of canola and olive oil for frying

Preheat the oven to 325°F. Season the short ribs with salt, pepper and coriander. In a large Dutch oven pot, heat both oils until shimmering. Sear the short ribs on all sides until browned. Remove from the pot and set aside. Sauté the onions until browned, about 8 min. Add the carrots, garlic, bay leaf and thyme and cook for another 5 min. Add the wine and reduce by 2/3. Add the tomatoes, beef stock and short ribs and let come to a boil.

Cover the pot, placing a layer of foil between the pot and the lid. Place the pot in the oven and braise for 2-2.5 hours. Take the pot out when the meat is almost falling off the bone and let sit at room temperature for 15 min. Remove the short ribs, strain the liquid and put it back in the pot.

Reduce until the flavor of the sauce is deepened but not too salty and concentrated. Check for seasoning and add the balsamic vinegar and parsley. Add the meat back to the pot, reheat and serve.

# Oven Baked Beef Casserole with Beets

### Serves 6-8

- 1½ lbs. ground beef
- 1 medium yellow onion, chopped
- 2-3 fresh beets, peeled and sliced
- 3 large fresh tomatoes
- 1-2 cups fresh Halloumi cheese (a white cheese from Cyprus)
- 3-4 tsp. coriander
- 3-4 tsp. paprika
- 3 tsp. cumin
- 2 tsp. cloves
- 1 tbsp. basil
- Sea salt and freshly ground black pepper

Preheat the oven to 400°F. Brown off the beef mince in a skillet with some olive oil and butter; when it is cooked thoroughly, add the onion and all spices except the basil to the skillet. Sauté for a few more minutes, then take half of the meat and cover the bottom of a medium-sized baking dish with edges.

Spread the sliced beets evenly over the beef mince, and top with the rest of the beef. Next, place the sliced tomatoes evenly on top and sprinkle the basil, salt and pepper over the tomatoes. Slice the Halloumi in ¼ inch slices and place over the tomatoes. Drizzle some olive oil on top of the cheese and bake in the oven for 20-25 min. The cheese should turn golden brown.

# BBQ Baby Back Ribs in Pineapple Glaze

### Serves 6-8

- 1-2 racks baby back ribs, cut between the bones
- ½ cored and trimmed pineapple, cut into ½ inch cubes
- 1 medium onion, finely chopped
- 4 cloves garlic, finely chopped or minced
- 1 6 oz. can tomato paste
- ½ cup tomato sauce
- 3 tbsp. Dijon mustard
- 4-5 tbsp. Worcestershire sauce
- 2-3 cups pineapple juice
- 3 tbsp. brown sugar
- 1-2 tbsp. smoked paprika
- 1 tbsp. ground coriander
- A pinch of cayenne pepper or chipotle
- Sea salt and freshly ground black pepper to taste

Sauté the onions in some canola oil and butter until translucent, add garlic and sauté for a few minutes longer. Add the tomato paste and while stirring, cook for 1 min. to cook off some of the acidity in the paste. Add the remaining ingredients and simmer for 5-10 min.

The sauce should be fairly thick to coat the ribs, but if too thick, add more pineapple juice.

Season the cut ribs with olive oil, salt, pepper and coriander and mark them on all sides on a hot grill. Place the grilled ribs tightly in a casserole, cover with the sauce and top with the chopped pineapple. Cover and braise on 300-325°F for about 2-2.5 hours.

After 1 hour, stir and rearrange the ribs as they will have shrunk. They should almost fall off the bone when done.

# Grandma's Beef Casserole

## Serves 6-8

- 1 lb. beef chuck, cut in 1 inch pieces (You can use a better cut of beef if you want.)
- 3 cups beef stock or vegetable stock
- 1 onion, chopped
- 1 large carrot, sliced
- 2 celery stalks, chopped
- ½ cup flour
- 3 tbsp. butter
- 3 bay leaves
- 2 tsp. coriander
- 1 tsp. cumin
- Sea salt and freshly ground black pepper to taste

Rinse the meat and pat dry. Add some salt and pepper to the flour, toss the meat in the flour and dust off. In a large pot, sear the meat with some of the butter and some olive oil; just make sure the pan is hot enough for the meat to brown nicely.

Remove the meat from the pan and sauté the prepared vegetables until soft, starting with the onions then carrots; add the spices to let them bloom. Add the meat back to the pot and pour all of the beef stock over, adding the bay leaves. Let come to a boil, reduce the heat and simmer on low heat for at least 1.5 hours, until the meat is very tender. Salt and pepper to taste and add a little more of the spices if needed. This dish is best served with potatoes or rice.

# My Bolognese

### Serves 6-8

- 2 lbs. ground beef
- 2 tbsp. olive oil, plus some canola oil
- 1 large onion, finely chopped
- 4 garlic cloves
- 1 6 oz. can of tomato paste
- 4 sprigs fresh thyme
- 3 sprigs fresh oregano
- 1 tbsp. dried oregano, the herbs tied together with some kitchen string
- 1 tbsp. smoked paprika
- 1 tbsp. ground coriander
- 1 cup red wine
- 1 12 oz. can good quality chopped tomatoes
- 1-2 cups beef stock
- Sea salt and freshly ground black pepper

Preheat the oven to 325°F. Heat a large, thick-bottomed skillet. When hot, add the olive and canola oils. When shimmering, take about 2 inch chunks of the ground beef and place in the hot pan. When browned on the bottom, turn the whole chunks over once.

When browned on both sides, use a hard, flat spatula to chop the chunks into smaller pieces in the pan. When almost cooked through, add the dry seasoning, including salt and pepper. Continue stirring/chopping until you have a fine and even mince. Remove the beef from the pan and transfer to a mixing bowl. Add some more of the oils to the pan and, when hot ,add the onions and sauté until translucent. Add the garlic and fresh herbs and sauté for 2 minutes more.

When fragrant, add the tomato paste and continue cooking while stirring for a few minutes. Add the wine and let come to a boil; the liquid will be very thick at this point. Add the beef stock, chopped tomatoes and the ground beef to the skillet. When it starts to simmer, cover the skillet and place in the oven. Let braise for an hour, stirring once. Check for seasoning and serve.

# Whole Roasted Tenderloin with Mustard and Thyme

### Serves 6-8

- 3 lbs. beef tenderloin, silver skin removed
- 3 tbsp. Dijon mustard
- 4 garlic cloves, minced
- 1 tbsp. fresh lemon juice
- 2 tbsp. fresh thyme, chopped
- ½ cup olive oil
- Sea salt and freshly ground black pepper

Preheat the oven to 450°F. Make small incisions along the grain all over the tenderloin using a paring knife, then place on a sheet pan. Prepare the marinade by whisking together the mustard, garlic, lemon juice, thyme and salt and pepper. Whisk in the oil in a slow stream until emulsified.

Check for seasoning and coat the tenderloin with the marinade, pressing some into the incisions. Cover with plastic wrap and let sit for an hour. Remove the plastic wrap and roast in the oven until a browned crust appears, about 15-20 min., then lower the heat to 350°F and continue roasting for another 10-15 min.

For medium doneness, pull the tenderloin out when the internal temperature in the thickest part reaches 120°F -125°F. When removed from the oven, cover with foil and let rest for 10 min so the carry-over cooking finishes and the juices are reintroduced to the meat. Slice and serve.

# Cottage Pie

## Serves 4-6

For the topping:
- 1 batch Duchesse potatoes (See index.)

For the filling:
- 2 lbs. ground beef
- 2 tbsp. canola oil
- 2 onions, finely chopped
- 3 garlic cloves, minced
- 3 thyme sprigs,
- 2 plum tomatoes, chopped
- 2 tbsp. tomato paste
- 1 ½ cups Guinness beer
- 4 tbsp. Worcestershire sauce
- 1 cup beef stock
- Sea salt and freshly ground black pepper

Preheat the oven to 350°F. In a thick-bottomed skillet, heat the canola oil until shimmering. Season the beef with salt and pepper and sear in 2 batches until nicely browned. Transfer the beef to a platter and set aside. Add more oil if necessary and sauté the onion; when softened, add the garlic and thyme. Sauté a few minutes more, stirring occasionally until browned.

Add the tomato paste and cook for a minute. Add the beef and the tomatoes to the pot and stir to combine. Add the Guinness and Worcestershire sauce, let come to a boil and reduce the liquid by half. Add the beef stock, reduce the heat and simmer for 25-30 min. until the mixture thickens. Check for seasoning and set aside. Make the Duchesse potatoes.

In a ceramic casserole, put an even layer of the beef mixture in the bottom. Spread an even layer of potato mixture on top of the beef and run over the surface with a fork. Add some more Parmesan on top and bake until golden brown, about 30 min. Let rest for 5 min. before serving.

# Pork Tenderloin in Sun-dried Tomato Sauce

**Serves 4-6**

- 1 whole pork tenderloin
- ½ cup sun-dried tomatoes, chopped
- 2 cups beef stock
- ½ cup crème fraiche
- 2 tbsp. soy sauce
- 2 tbsp. butter
- 2 tbsp. olive oil
- 4 garlic cloves, chopped
- Sea salt and pepper to taste

Start by cleaning the meat of excess fat. This is best done with a thin, sharp knife. Just make a small cut at the end, pull the fat up and continue to pull as you cut. Cut the tenderloin into ½ inch pieces and set aside while you chop the sun-dried tomatoes and garlic.

Heat a skillet with the olive oil and butter, add the meat and brown about 2-3 min. on each side. Lower the heat, add the garlic and sun-dried tomatoes and cook for a few minutes. Pour in the soy sauce and stir. Add the stock and let simmer for 10 min. Add the crème fraiche, salt and pepper and let simmer for another 5-10 min. Best served with rice or potatoes.

# Daniel's Swedish Meatballs

### Serves 6-8

- 1 lb. lean ground beef
- ½ lb. ground pork (optional)
- ½ cup oats or bread crumbs
- ¼ cup cream
- 1 yellow onion, grated
- 2 cloves garlic
- 3 tbsp. butter
- 2 whole eggs, lightly whisked
- 3-4 tsp. allspice
- 2-3 tsp. paprika
- 2 tsp. freshly ground black pepper
- 2 tsp. sea salt

This is the secret recipe for classic traditional Swedish meatballs. I could not count how many times I have brought these to a party with immense success; I have to say that they have almost reached the standard of my Grandmother's, but I will never get there.

Start by soaking the oats with the cream for 5 min., then add the grated onion, which can be done by hand with a grater, or in a food processor. Add the spices and leave for another 3 min.

Blend in the ground meat with your hands and add the eggs. Be careful not to overwork the mix, as the meat will turn stringy. The batter should be quite moist for the meatballs to come out juicy. Let rest 10 min. at room temperature before shaping into small balls with your hands.

A round scoop or melon baller may also be used if desired. Alternately, small patties can be made to save time. Cook a small piece to test the flavor and spices. Heat a large skillet, add the butter and wait until the pan is very hot and the butter becomes nut colored. Fill the pan with meatballs and turn them once with a fork to brown them on both sides. Next, start giving the pan a 'shake' once in a while to complete the cooking process. You will know they are done by feeling if they are somewhat firm or by cutting one in half. They are traditionally served with mashed potatoes and cream sauce.

# Grilled Pork Chops with Adobo

### Serves 4-6

- 2 lbs. pork chops, thin cut
- 1 tbsp. fresh lemon juice
- 1 tbsp. white wine vinegar
- 2 garlic cloves, minced
- 1 tbsp. Dijon mustard
- 1 tsp. dried oregano
- 2 tbsp. adobo spice blend
- 5 tbsp. olive oil
- Sea salt and freshly ground black pepper to taste

Combine all ingredients except the olive oil in a mixing bowl. Whisk in the olive oil in a slow stream until combined and emulsified. Check for seasoning and submerge the pork chops fully.

Let marinade for 1-24 hours. Heat a grill to high heat. Scrape the grid with a wire brush, dip a kitchen towel in some canola oil and coat the surface of the grill with it. Sear the pork chops on the grill until nice grill marks appear.

After turning the meat over, close the lid of the grill, checking occasionally until fully cooked.

# Braised lamb with Carrots

## Serves 4-6

- 1 ½ lbs. lamb shank, trimmed of excess fat and cut into ½ inch cubes
- 2 onions, coarsely chopped
- 5 garlic cloves, minced
- 2 celery ribs, coarsely chopped
- 6 carrots, peeled and whole
- 1 cup red wine
- ½ cup port wine
- 3-4 cups beef stock
- 2 rosemary sprigs
- ¼ cup fresh parsley, finely chopped
- Canola oil for sautéing
- Sea salt and freshly ground black pepper to taste

Preheat the oven to 325°F. Season the lamb with salt and pepper. In a large Dutch oven pot, heat some canola oil until shimmering. Sear the lamb on all sides over high heat until browned. Using a slotted spoon, remove the lamb from the pot and reheat, adding more oil if necessary. Sauté the onions with some salt; when soft, reduce the heat, add the garlic and stir for a minute. Add the celery and continue cooking for a few minutes. Add the wine and the port and cook until reduced by half. Add the rosemary, carrots and the lamb to the pot and fill with beef stock until just covered.

Let come to a boil, cover and put the pot in the oven. Braise for at least 2 hours, stirring gently once, until the lamb is very tender. Take the pot out of the oven and let rest at room temp for 20 min. Transfer the lamb and carrots to a platter and cover. Strain the liquid and put it back into the pot. Reduce it to about 2 cups. Taste first and season with salt and pepper and the fresh parsley. Add the carrots and lamb back to the pot to reheat and serve. Alternately, place the lamb over the carrots on a serving platter and spoon over the sauce.

# Lamb Curry

## Serves 4-6

- 1 lb. ground lamb
- 3 cloves garlic, chopped
- 2 tbsp. soy sauce
- 2-3 tbsp. curry powder
- 2 tbsp. paprika

Brown the lamb in some olive oil and butter, add the garlic and spices and cook for a few minutes more, then add the soy sauce. Serve as is over rice or quinoa. Note: The lamb can be replaced with any ground meat. It is also very easy to make a sauce with it; just add 2 cups of coconut milk and simmer for a few minutes.

# Poultry

Chicken and other poultry are among the leanest and most versatile sources of protein. The cooking variations are endless and it is easy to prepare and to make in bigger batches; just do not overcook it as it gets dry easily. Chicken will provide you with a healthy lunch the day after, since it stays fresh and tasty for a reasonably long time after being cooked. You can intentionally make more than you need to freeze or, for example, to use in a chicken salad or blend into a casserole. Always be sure to choose free range, organic chicken and poultry to be certain that they have had a happy and hormone-free life with all the necessary exercise and movement.

# Moroccan Turkey Meatballs with Tahini Sauce

## Serves 4-6

### For Meatballs:
- 2 lbs. ground turkey
- ½ yellow onion
- 2 garlic cloves
- 1 tbsp. fresh ginger
- 1 tsp. coriander
- 1 tsp. cumin
- 2 tbsp. lemon juice
- ½ cup panko bread crumbs
- ¼ cup cream
- 2 eggs
- ½ bunch fresh cilantro
- Sea salt and freshly ground black pepper

### For Tahini sauce:
- 1 cup tahini
- ¼ cup fresh lemon juice
- 1 small garlic clove
- 1 tsp. cumin
- Sea salt and freshly ground black pepper to taste
- Water A/N

Preheat the oven to 450°F. To make the meatballs, combine the onion, garlic and ginger in a food processor and run until coarsely chopped. Add the dry spices, bread crumbs, lemon juice and cream and pulse until well-combined. Add the eggs and pulse again.

Add the cilantro and pulse until the leaves are coarsely chopped. Use your hand to combine the mixture with the turkey, being careful not to overwork the meat. Let the flavors combine for 10 min. and test fry a small piece in a skillet with some oil to check the seasoning. Roll small meatballs with your hands and place on an oiled sheet pan. Roast the meatballs for 8-10 min. until well-browned and cooked through.

To make the sauce: Pulse the garlic in a food processor first. Add the remaining ingredients except the water and pulse to combine. Add the water while the processor is running until the desired consistency is achieved; it should be fairly thick but not chunky.

Check for seasoning and drizzle over the hot meatballs.

# The Best Roasted Chicken

**Serves 4**

- 1 whole fryer chicken
- 1 stick butter, softened
- 2 garlic cloves, minced
- 1 tbsp. dried Italian herbs
- 1 orange, halved
- 1 lemon, halved
- 1 onion, coarsely chopped
- 3 sprigs each fresh thyme, rosemary, marjoram and sage
- Sea salt and freshly ground black pepper A/N

Rinse the chicken and pat dry. Combine the butter, garlic, herbs, salt and pepper. Loosen the skin of the chicken breast by carefully running your finger under the skin. Spread a dollop of the butter mixture over the entire breast under the skin. Add olive oil, salt and pepper to the cavity and fill up with the other ingredients in the following order: herbs, ½ lemon, ½ orange (squeezing to release the juice), and onion.

Use the excess skin to 'close' the cavity. Squeeze the remaining juice over the top of the chicken and add olive oil, salt and pepper and more Italian herbs. Roast at 400°F for 15 min. then lower the heat to 350°F and roast for another 30 min. or so. Check the temperature of the breast with a thermometer and pull it out when it reaches 160°F. Cover with foil and let rest for 10-15 min before slicing.

# Chicken Stroganoff

**Serves 4-6**

- 2 lbs. boneless skinless chicken breast, cut into thin strips
- 2 tbsp. canola oil
- 1 onion, finely chopped
- 2 tbsp. flour
- 2-3 tbsp. tomato paste
- 2 tbsp. Dijon mustard
- 2 cups chicken stock
- 1 cup cream
- Sea salt and freshly ground black pepper

In a thick-bottomed casserole, sauté the chicken strips over high heat with the canola oil until browned, adding some salt and pepper. Remove the chicken, add more oil if necessary and sauté the onions until translucent. Add the flour and cook for a minute while stirring. Add the chicken stock , tomato paste and mustard and stir to dissolve. Let the liquid reduce under a soft boil for 5-10 min. and check if more tomato paste or mustard is required. Add the cream and cook for another 10 min. until slightly thickened. Add the chicken and season with salt and pepper to taste.

# Chicken Piccata

**Serves 4-6**

- 4 boneless skinless chicken breasts, trimmed and cut lengthwise
- All-purpose flour for dredging
- 1 onion, finely chopped
- 6 tbsp. unsalted butter
- Olive oil A/N
- 1 cup chicken stock
- ½ cup lemon juice
- ½ cup brined capers
- ⅓ cup parsley, finely chopped
- Sea salt and freshly ground black pepper

Season the chicken with salt and pepper. Dredge in flour and shake off the excess.

In a large skillet, heat the butter with some olive oil and brown the chicken pieces on both sides. Remove and set on a platter. Add more butter and sauté the onions, scraping up the brown bits. Add the chicken stock and reduce the liquid by half. Add the chicken, lemon juice and capers to the pan and simmer for 5 min. Swirl in chunks of cold butter until the sauce has thickened slightly. Finally, add the parsley and check for seasoning.

# The Best Grilled Chicken Breast

**Serves 4-6**

- 4 large chicken breasts, cleaned and cut lengthwise
- 4 tbsp. paprika powder
- 4 tbsp. granulated garlic
- 1 tbsp. tomato paste
- 1 tsp. red wine vinegar
- 1 tbsp. tamari or soy sauce
- Sea salt and freshly ground black pepper
- Olive oil A/N

Combine all ingredients except the olive oil in a bowl. Slowly whisk in the olive oil until a fairly thick paste forms. Check for seasoning and fold the chicken breast well to coat in the marinade. Let marinate for 1-24 hours. Heat a grill and sear on high heat for grill marks and flavor. When both sides are marked, reduce the heat on the grill, and close the lid and cook until done. Alternately, finish the cooking process in a 350°F oven for 5-10 min.

# Saffron and Lemon Braised Chicken

## Serves 4-6

- 4 chicken drumsticks
- 4 chicken thighs
- 4 tbsp. butter or olive oil
- 1 onion, finely chopped
- 1 garlic clove, minced
- 1 tbsp. fresh ginger, minced
- ½ tsp. saffron
- 1 cinnamon stick
- 2-3 cups chicken stock
- 1 14 oz. can chopped tomatoes
- 1 preserved lemon (or regular), seeds removed and chopped
- 1 can garbanzo beans
- ¼ cup fresh parsley, finely chopped
- Sea salt and freshly ground black pepper

Season the chicken pieces with salt and pepper. In a deep casserole or Dutch oven, sear the chicken on both sides over high heat. When browned, remove the chicken and put on a platter. Add more butter or oil if necessary and sauté the onions with a sprinkle of salt until softened; add the garlic and ginger and sauté until fragrant. Add the saffron and cinnamon stick and stir quickly before adding the chicken stock, tomatoes and preserved lemon.

Let come to a boil and add the chicken pieces back in and submerge in the liquid. Cover and let simmer over low heat or in the oven at 325°F for 40-45 min. until very tender. Meanwhile, rinse the garbanzos and remove loose skins. Add the garbanzos to the chicken as well as the parsley. Simmer uncovered for 15 min. for the flavors to merge and the sauce to reduce a bit. Check the seasoning and serve with rice or couscous.

# Chicken with Sun-Dried Tomato Pesto

### Serves 6-8

- 1 cup sun-dried tomatoes in oil, drained
- ¾ cup grated Parmesan cheese
- 1 cup fresh basil
- 3 garlic cloves
- 3 tbsp. pine nuts
- ¾ cup olive oil
- 2 cups crème fraiche
- 3 lbs. skinless chicken pieces, thighs and breast

Preheat the oven to 350°F. To make the pesto, pulse the first 5 ingredients in a food processor until smooth. With the processor running, add the olive oil in a slow stream until a paste forms.

Combine the pesto and crème fraiche with some salt and pepper in a mixing bowl and toss it with the chicken. Place the chicken in an even layer in a ceramic baking dish.

Cover with foil and bake in the oven for about 30 min. or until the chicken is done.

# Grilled Chicken with Mustard and Tarragon

**Serves 4-6**

- 1 whole fresh chicken
- 4 tbsp. butter or ghee
- 1-2 tbsp. Dijon mustard
- 2 tbsp. dried tarragon
- 3 tsp. sea salt

Preheat the oven to 300°F. Carefully melt the butter in a small saucepan and mix in the mustard and tarragon. Brush over the chicken and bake for about 2 hours until golden brown. Test the internal temperature of the breast; it should reach 160°F. Take the chicken out of the oven and let rest for 15 min. covered before slicing.

# Chicken Curry

**Serves 4-6**

- 1½ lbs. chicken breast fillets, sliced into 2 thinner pieces or cubes
- 1 large carrot, grated
- 1 medium onion, chopped
- 2 cloves garlic, minced
- 1 tbsp. fresh ginger, minced
- 1 cup cashews, coarsely chopped (optional)
- 1 cup fresh pineapple, chopped (optional)
- 2 cups chicken stock
- 1 cup coconut milk
- 2 tbsp. curry powder
- 1 tbsp. turmeric

Cut the chicken into the desired shape and brown the pieces in a medium-sized pot on high heat with some coconut oil. Only turn them once so that the juices stay inside the meat. Take the chicken out and set aside. Add some more coconut oil to the pot and gently sauté the onion and carrot.

After 3-5 min., add the garlic, ginger, curry and turmeric. Allow the flavors to bloom for about a minute, then add the chicken stock. Let simmer on low heat for 10-15 min. When the vegetables have simmered in the stock for 10-15 min., add the chicken, cashews and coconut milk. Simmer for another 5-10 min, checking the chicken occasionally to make sure it is cooked through. Turn the heat off and let rest for 5 min. before serving. You can also replace the nuts with some chopped chili and shrimp.

# Lemon and Herb Grilled Chicken Breast

### Serves 4-6

- 4 large chicken breasts, cleaned and cut lengthwise
- 4 garlic cloves
- 2 tbsp. lemon juice
- 2 tbsp. fresh thyme, leaves only
- 2 tbsp. fresh rosemary, leaves only
- Olive oil A/N
- Sea salt and freshly ground black pepper

In a food processor, pulse the garlic until chopped. Scrape down from the sides and add the lemon juice, herbs and some salt and pepper. With the processor running, slowly add olive oil until thickened and emulsified.

Taste to check the balance between the acid in the lemon and the oil and add more if necessary. Toss the chicken in the marinade, cover and let marinate for 1-24 hours.

Heat a grill and sear on high heat for grill marks and flavor. When both sides are marked, reduce the heat on the grill, close the lid and cook until done. Alternately, finish the cooking process in a 350°F oven for 5-10 min.

# Chicken Stir-Fry

## Serves 4-6

- 1½ lbs. chicken breast fillet
- 1 batch meat marinade excluding the wine and sun-dried tomatoes (Optional, see index.)
- 1 green pepper, sliced lengthwise
- 1 halved carrot, sliced lengthwise into strips
- 1 medium onion, sliced
- 3 tbsp. tamari
- 2 tbsp. herbs de Provence
- 3 tsp. sea salt

Cut the chicken into ½ inch pieces or strips or as desired. Marinade the chicken and let sit for a while at room temperature. Heat 2 skillets with olive oil and butter. Add the chicken to one and the vegetables to the other. Stir the vegetables occasionally. The chicken should be lightly browned before taken off the heat. When the vegetables are browned and softened, add the herbs, then the tamari. Add the chicken to the vegetables and season with sea salt.

# Chicken in Lemon and Cilantro Sauce with Olives

## Serves 6-8

- 2 lbs. chicken breast fillet
- 1 ½ cups vegetable or chicken stock
- ¾ cup cream
- 1 onion, chopped
- 4 cloves garlic, chopped
- 1 cup green pitted olives, sliced
- 1 cup fresh cilantro, chopped
- ½ cup dry white wine
- Juice of 1 lemon
- Sea salt and pepper

Cut the chicken in halves to make 2 thinner pieces of each fillet. Make a marinade out of olive oil, paprika, salt and pepper and let the chicken marinade for a while before browning them off.

In the same skillet, sauté the onions for a few minutes, then add the garlic and some salt and pepper. Pour in the white wine and cook for 1 min.; add the stock and cream and let reduce for 20 min. Add the olives and chicken and simmer for another 5 min. Lastly, add the cilantro and lemon juice before serving.

# Chicken in Tomato Sauce with Olives and Capers

### Serves 6-8

- 2 lbs. chicken breast fillets
- 2 batches basic tomato sauce (See index.)
- 1 cup mixed pitted olives, halved
- ½ cup capers
- ½ cup fresh oregano

Cut the chicken in ½ inch pieces and brown them while the tomato sauce is simmering. Add the olives and capers to the tomato sauce when it's done. When the sauce is ready, add the chicken to the pot as well as the fresh oregano. Simmer for a few minutes more then add salt and pepper to taste. This dish is great served with saffron rice.

# Mango Chicken

### Serves 4-6

- 1½ lbs. chicken breast fillets
- ½ onion, chopped
- 1 ripe mango, cut into pieces
- ¾ cup dried apricots
- 2 cups chicken stock
- 1 bag arugula
- Sea salt and pepper

Cut each fillet into about 3 pieces, brown in a pan and put aside. Add the chopped onions and sauté them in the same pan in some more olive oil, add the stock and simmer for 5 min. Add the chicken, mango and apricots and simmer for an additional 5-10 min. Turn off the heat, add the arugula and leave for a few minutes before serving.

# Chicken Roulades

### Serves 4-6

- 1 lb. chicken breast fillets
- 6-8 slices of ham
- 4 tbsp. Dijon mustard
- ½ cup feta cheese
- Olive oil and butter for sautéing
- Sea salt and pepper
- Toothpicks

Cut the chicken breasts in halves horizontally to make 2 thinner fillets from each piece. Pound with a mallet if still too thick. Place them on a sheet pan and spread mustard on one side of each piece. Add one slice of ham to each chicken fillet, followed by some feta cheese and salt and pepper.

Roll the pieces from the small end of the chicken into roulades, holding them together with toothpicks. Heat a skillet with the oil and butter and sauté your roulades one side at a time.

After they are evenly browned, lower the heat, cover and cook until thoroughly done. They can also be covered and placed in the oven to cook through. When ready, sprinkle some salt and pepper on top and serve.

An alternative filling is wilted spinach, roasted bell peppers and blanched asparagus.

# Italian Chicken Meatballs

**Serves 4-6**

- 1 lb. ground chicken
- ½ cup ground oats or bread crumbs
- 2 whole eggs
- 3 tablespoons of cream
- ½ cup grated Parmesan
- 2 tsp. garlic powder
- 2 tsp. Italian herbs
- Sea salt and freshly ground black pepper

In a mixing bowl, blend the oats, cream, eggs and spices and let rest for 5 min. Put the chicken in the bowl and mix with hands; lastly, add the cheese, cover and let rest for 10 min. Form somewhat large balls with your hands and brown off in a skillet. Alternately, they can be baked in the oven for 20-25 min. at 400°F. They can also be served in 1 batch of basic tomato sauce (See index.).

# Turkey in Green Pepper Sauce

**Serves 4-6**

- 1 lb. turkey breast fillet
- 1 onion, sliced
- 2 garlic cloves, smashed
- 1 cup vegetable stock
- 1 cup cream
- 1 tbsp. crushed green pepper
- Sea salt

Cut the turkey in ½ inch pieces and brown them in a skillet with some olive oil and butter. Remove the turkey and add the onions and garlic to the pot and cook for a few minutes more.

Add a generous amount of crushed green pepper, followed by the stock. Let the stock reduce for about 10-15 min., then add the cream. Let the cream reduce for about 10 min.; add the turkey back into the pot and simmer for 5 min. Add sea salt to taste.

# Thanksgiving Brined Turkey

## Serves 16-20

1 16-18 lb. turkey

For the brine:
- 2 oranges
- 2 lemons
- 1 bunch each thyme and rosemary
- 2 bay leaves
- ½ - 1 cup of sugar
- 1 cup sea salt
- 1 tbsp. freshly ground black pepper corn
- ½ cup orange tequila or other liqueur (optional)
- 1 gallon water or A/N
- 3 cups vegetable stock

For the stuffing:
- 1 bunch each thyme, rosemary, sage, marjoram
- 1 onion, coarsely chopped
- 1 carrot, coarsely chopped
- ½ lemon
- ½ orange
- 3 tbsp. butter, softened
- Sea salt and freshly ground black pepper

Combine the liquids with the salt and sugar and whisk to dissolve. Slice the orange and the lemon in half, squeeze the juice into the liquid and add the rinds, followed by the rest of the ingredients. Put the liquid into a large brining bag and fully submerge the turkey in it. Refrigerate and let marinade for 24-48 hours, turning the turkey over once halfway.

Remove the turkey from the brine and pat dry, discard the brine. Stuff the turkey with the herbs, orange, lemon, carrot and onion. Coat the outside of the bird all over with the softened butter and sprinkle an even layer of salt and pepper. Roast the turkey at 500°F in the lower part of the oven for 30 min., then reduce the heat to 350°F and roast until a thermometer reads 161°F in the thickest part of the breast.

Calculate about 20 min. per pound; for example, a 16 pound bird should roast for 2-2 ½ hours. Cover with foil if it get too much color. Let rest at room temperature for 15-20 min. before carving.

# Turkey Burgers

**Serves 4-6**

- 1½ lbs. dark turkey meat, ground
- ½ cup ground oats or bread crumbs
- 2 whole eggs
- 1 red onion, finely chopped
- 1 cup cilantro
- 2 tbsp. curry powder
- Sea salt and freshly ground black pepper

In a mixing bowl, blend oats, eggs, onions and spices, then add the turkey and let combine for at least 10 min. Form patties with your hands and put on a sheet pan. Heat some olive oil and butter in a pan, brown them on each side for 2-3 min. and lower the heat to cook through.

# Turkey Chili

**Serves 6-8**

- 2 lbs. turkey, ground
- 2 batches basic tomato sauce with tomato paste
- 2 tbsp. taco or fajita seasoning
- 1 can pinto beans
- 1 can kidney beans
- 1 chopped chili pepper or jalapeno (optional)
- 1-2 cups chicken stock, more if needed
- Sea salt and pepper

Make the tomato sauce, adding the chopped chili peppers with the onion. As it simmers, brown the ground turkey. Take half of the pinto beans and mush into pulp with a fork or in a food processor. After the turkey is browned and while still in the pan, sprinkle salt, pepper and the seasoning and add the tomato sauce along with the beans. Let simmer for about 10 min. Serve with rice or quinoa.

# Coconut Turkey

## Serves 4-6

- 1½ lbs. ground turkey
- 1 cup vegetable broth
- 1 cup coconut milk
- 1 carrot, grated
- ½ onion, chopped
- ½ red pepper, chopped
- 1 tomato, finely chopped
- 2 tbsp. curry powder
- Juice of ½ lemon plus the zest

Brown the turkey in a deep skillet. Remove and then sauté the vegetables except for the tomatoes, onions and peppers first, then the carrots. When the vegetables are soft, add the curry powder and tomato and stir. Add the vegetable stock. Let simmer for 10 min. before adding the turkey and coconut milk, then let simmer for another 5-7 min. Squeeze in the lemon and the zest, turn off the heat and let rest for 3 min. before serving.

# Fish & Seafood

Fish is a great source of protein that is easy to digest and assimilate. One should eat fish once or twice a week. Just make sure you get wild caught and not farm-raised, as there is a higher probability that they contain mercury and other toxic heavy metals.

# Slow Poached Salmon in Dill and Cider Vinegar Broth

**Serves 4-6**

- 2 lbs. salmon fillet, skin removed and cut into equal-size pieces
- 10 cups water
- 2 cups apple cider vinegar
- 1 cup sugar, (or more to taste)
- 2 bunches of fresh dill
- 2 lemons
- 1 tbsp. fennel seeds
- 1 tbsp. anise seeds
- 2 tbsp. sea salt

Preheat the oven to 225°F. In a large pot, combine all ingredients except the salmon and let come to a boil. Whisk until the sugar is dissolved and check the seasoning balance; it should be both sweet and sour. Remove from the heat and let cool slightly.

Place the pieces of salmon in a deep ceramic casserole and season with salt and pepper. Pour the liquid over the fish and cover with foil. Poach the salmon in the oven for 20 min.; check for doneness and keep the salmon in the liquid until served. Alternately, cut smaller pieces of the salmon and when done and cooled, refrigerate in the liquid. It can be kept overnight and served cold as an appetizer.

# Grilled Swordfish

**Serves 4-6**

- 4-6 pieces swordfish, 1 inch thick
- 4 cloves garlic, chopped
- 1 bunch cilantro, chopped
- Juice of one lemon
- ½ cup olive oil
- 1 tsp. freshly ground black pepper

Mix the ingredients for the marinade and put in the swordfish to marinade for at least 10 min. Grill them quickly on a hot grill, turning them only once. Serve immediately.

# Sesame Seed Roasted Salmon in Lemon Marinade

**Serves 4-6**

- 1½ lbs. salmon, sliced in 1 inch pieces
- 4 tbsp. olive oil
- ½ - ¾ cup black and white sesame seeds
- Juice of 1 lemon
- Sea salt and freshly ground black pepper

Make a marinade with the olive oil, lemon juice, salt and pepper and let the salmon sit in it for a few minutes.

Pour the sesame seeds on a flat plate, and dip it each piece of the salmon into the seeds on the side opposite of the skin. Heat a skillet with some butter and olive oil and sear the side with the skin first.

After 3 min. or so, turn them over carefully so the seeds remain on the surface; peel off the skin with a fork, or leave on if desired. Turn them over again in order to not brown the seeds too much and cook on low heat until done. You can also cover the pan with a lid or put the pan in the oven for a few minutes.

# Poppy Seed Salmon with Orange Soy Glaze

### Serves 4-6

- 6 square pieces wild caught salmon, skin removed
- Poppy seeds A/N
- 2 cups freshly squeezed orange juice
- 1 tbsp. tamari or soy sauce
- 2 tbsp. cold butter or more if needed
- Sea salt and freshly ground freshly ground black pepper
- Olive oil A/N
- Canola oil A/N

Preheat the oven to 350°F. Put the orange juice in a pot and start reducing it down to ½ cup; it should be thick at this point. Whisk in the soy sauce followed by mounting butter until it forms a thick glaze.

Coat the salmon with olive oil and sprinkle with salt and pepper. Pour some poppy seeds on a plate and press the top side of the salmon only onto the plate, creating an even layer of poppy seeds.

Heat a skillet with some canola oil until the oil is shimmering. Sear the bottom only of the salmon until browned and transfer to a sheet pan.

When all pieces are seared, put the sheet pan with the salmon into the oven and finish the cooking until the desired doneness is reached, about 5-10 min. Place the salmon on a plate and pour the sauce over. Serve immediately.

# Slow Roasted Salmon with Citrus And Herbs

### Serves 6-8

- 1 whole piece salmon, about 3 lbs.
- 6 tbsp. butter, softened
- 4 medium shallots, finely chopped
- 3 cloves garlic, minced
- 3 tbsp. fresh tarragon, finely chopped
- 3 tbsp. fresh marjoram, finely chopped
- Zest and juice of 2 lemons
- Juice of 1 orange
- 2 tsp. sea salt
- 2 tsp. freshly ground black pepper
- A pinch of cayenne pepper
- Olive oil A/N

Preheat the oven to 300°F. Combine all ingredients except the salmon in a mixing bowl and let sit for 20 min. at room temperature. Rinse the salmon and pat dry. Drizzle some olive oil in non-reactive baking dish, big enough to fit the whole salmon.

Place the salmon skin down in the baking dish and spread the seasoning mixture over in an even layer. Pour the orange juice around the fish and cover with aluminum foil. Bake in the middle of the oven for about 25-30 min. until the salmon is opaque in the center when pierced with a paring knife.

# Roasted Salmon

### Serves 4-6

- 4-6 pieces salmon, 1½ inch cut
- 4 tbsp. olive oil
- 2-3 tbsp. lemon pepper
- 3 tsp. sea salt

With dill:
- ½ cup fresh dill, chopped
- Juice of 1 lemon

Or, with sun-dried tomatoes, feta cheese and olives:
- ½ cup sun-dried tomatoes, sliced
- ½ cup Kalamata olives, chopped
- ½ cup feta cheese, crumbled

Preheat oven to 375°F. In a mixing bowl, combine the olive oil with the lemon pepper, salt and half of the lemon juice and marinade the salmon for 10 min. Transfer to a baking dish and bake in the oven for 20-25 min. Take it out and sprinkle the dill over the salmon, followed by the rest of the lemon juice.

For the sun-dried tomatoes option, cut small pockets in the sides of the fish, stuff them with the sun-dried tomatoes, olives and the feta cheese and follow the above procedure.

# Ginger Basil Salmon

**Serves 6-8**

- 2 lbs. skinless fresh salmon, cut into cubes
- 2 cups vegetable stock
- 3 tbsp. coconut oil (olive oil can be used)
- 2 cans coconut milk
- 1 fennel, chopped
- 4 shallots, finely chopped
- 4 cloves garlic, chopped
- 4 tbsp. ginger, freshly grated
- 1 cup of fresh basil, thinly sliced
- Juice of 2 limes

Sauté the fennel and shallots in the coconut oil for a few minutes in a large pot then, while stirring, add the ginger and garlic. Sprinkle some salt and pepper over, add the vegetable stock and let simmer for 10-15 min. Add the coconut milk and simmer for another 5 min.

In a thick-bottomed skillet, sear the salmon pieces on high heat, turning only once. Be careful so that they do not fall apart. Add the salmon to the pot with vegetables and leave for a few minutes before adding the lime juice and basil. Season with salt and pepper to taste.

# Whole Grilled Salmon with Paprika And Herbs

**Serves 6-8**

- 1 whole piece salmon, skin on, approximately 2.5-3 lbs.
- Olive oil A/N
- 2 tbsp. fresh lemon juice
- Pimenton paprika A/N
- Dried Italian herbs A/N
- Sea salt and freshly ground black pepper to taste

Preheat a grill to high heat. Starting on the top side of the fish, drizzle olive oil in an even layer, followed by half of the lemon juice. Sprinkle an even layer of the paprika and then the Italian herbs, salt and pepper. Place the whole fish on a piece of foil and repeat the process on the skin side of the fish. Holding both ends of the foil, transfer the entire fish on to the grill and grill until you see the bottom turning solid pink 1/3 of the way up the side.

Remove from grill and using two thick spatulas, carefully turn the fish over on the foil. It should have nice grill marks on the top side. Return the fish to the grill and repeat the process until fully cooked through. If it gets too much color, place the fish, foil and all, on a sheet pan and finish the cooking process in the oven at 350°F.

# Saffron, Tomato and Orange White Fish

**Serves 4-6**

- 1-2 lbs. white fish fillets, skin removed and cut into 2x2 inch squares
- 1 cup mayonnaise
- 2 tbsp. tomato paste
- 4 tbsp. freshly squeezed orange juice
- ½ tsp. saffron
- Sea salt and freshly ground black pepper to taste

Combine the ingredients for the marinade and check the seasoning. Coat the fish well with the sauce and marinade in the refrigerator for 1 hour. Preheat the oven to 400°F. Place the fish on a sheet pan and roast for about 10-15 min., depending on thickness. Check the doneness by cutting through a piece or poking it with your finger. It should be soft to the touch while slightly firm. Be careful not to overcook!

# Miso Glazed Sea Bass

**Serves 4-6**

- 6 pieces sea bass, skin removed
- ½ cup yellow miso paste
- ¼ cup mirin or sake
- 1 garlic clove, minced
- 1 tsp. ground ginger
- 1 tsp. brown sugar
- 1 tsp. red chili flakes
- ½ cup sesame oil
- ¼ cup canola oil
- Freshly ground black pepper

Preheat the oven to 450°F. Whisk together all ingredients except the oils. Slowly whisk in the oils until a smooth sauce-like consistency appears. Check for seasoning and add more oil if necessary (the miso is very salty). Submerge the fish in the marinade and let sit for at least 1 hour or overnight if possible. Place the fish pieces on a sheet pan and roast until the corners start to blacken. Check for doneness by piercing with a sharp knife.

# Steamed halibut in Banana Leaf with Gremolata

**Serves 4-6**

- 2 lbs. fresh halibut, skin removed, cut into medium squares
- 6 banana leaves (or parchment paper)

For the gremolata:
- 1 tbsp. grated lemon zest
- 4 garlic cloves, minced
- ½ cup fresh parsley, finely chopped
- 2 tbsp. fresh lemon juice
- ¼ cup olive oil or A/N
- Sea salt and freshly ground black pepper to taste

Combine all the ingredients for the gremolata in a mixing bowl except the olive oil. Slowly whisk in the olive oil until emulsified. Cut approximately 5 x 5 inch pieces out of the banana leaf. Place the pieces of fish in the center of each leaf then spread an even layer of gremolata on top. Fold the lower side first, followed by the upper side of the leaf, then tuck the sides under the fish. Place the parcels in a steaming basket or pot. Cover and steam for about 10-15 min. until done.

# Cod in Parsley Parcel

**Serves 4-6**

- 2 cod fillets
- 4 tbsp. butter or ghee
- 1 cup fresh parsley, chopped
- Juice of 1 lemon
- 2 tsp. freshly ground black pepper
- Sea salt

Preheat the oven to 375°F. Prepare a baking dish with two layers of aluminum foil, one lengthwise and one widthwise. Rinse and dry the cod; sprinkle salt and pepper on both sides of the fillets and place them next to each other on the foil. Top with knobs of butter, followed by the parsley and lemon juice. Fold and close the edges of the foil over the fish and bake in the oven for 25 min. Open the parcel and make a small cut in the fish; when it is white all the way through, it is ready.

# Sake and Mirin Steamed Sea Bass

### Serves 4-6

- 6 pieces sea bass, skin removed
- ½ cup each tarragon, chervil, thyme and marjoram
- ½ cup toasted sesame oil
- ½ cup dry sake
- ½ cup mirin (sweet Asian cooking wine)
- Sea salt and freshly ground black pepper
- Toasted black sesame seeds, A/N

Preheat the oven to 350°F. In a ceramic roasting pan, cover the bottom with the fresh herbs and place the pieces of fish over it with some space in between.

Drizzle the sake and mirin all over the fish, followed by the sesame oil. Season with salt and pepper and sprinkle the sesame seeds on top. Cover the dish with foil and cook in the oven for 15-20 min. until just done. Let rest a few minutes before serving.

# Tuna Salad

**Serves 1-2**

- 1 can good quality tuna
- ¼ fennel, finely chopped
- 1 celery rib, finely chopped
- ¼ cup green onions, diced
- 3-4 tbsp. mayonnaise
- 2 tbsp. yogurt
- Juice of ½ lemon
- 3 tsp. lemon pepper
- 3 tsp. oregano
- 1-2 tsp. sea salt

OR

- ¼ cup red onion, diced
- 3-4 tbsp. mayonnaise
- 2 tbsp. yogurt
- 1 hardboiled egg, diced
- Juice of ½ lemon
- 3 tsp. lemon pepper
- 3 tbsp. fresh dill
- 1-2 tsp. sea salt

Blend all ingredients in bowl with a fork and let sit for a few minutes before serving. This recipe can easily be doubled.

# Tuna Stuffed Bell Peppers

**Serves 4**

- 2 cans tuna
- 2 red bell peppers
- ½ cup pesto
- 1 tomato, finely chopped
- ½ cup mozzarella cheese
- Sea salt and pepper

Preheat the oven to 400°F. Cut the peppers in half, removing the seeds and pith but keeping the stem. Chop the tomatoes fine and mix them with the tuna, pesto and spices. Stuff each pepper with the mixture, sprinkle the cheese on top and bake in the oven for 20-25 min. until the cheese is golden brown.

## Whitefish in Pepper in Avocado Sauce

**Serves 4-6**

- 1 lb. firm whitefish
- 1 cup vegetable stock
- ¾ cup cream
- ½ yellow pepper, sliced
- 2 cloves garlic, chopped
- ½ avocado, cubed
- Sea salt and freshly ground black pepper

Sauté the pepper with the garlic in some olive oil for a few minutes, then add the stock and cream and let simmer for another couple of minutes. Add the fish and let simmer a little longer. Lastly, when cooked, add the avocado, turn off the heat and sprinkle on some salt and pepper to taste.

## Whitefish Medley

**Serves 4-6**

- 1 lb. snapper
- ½ fennel, sliced
- 1 large carrot, grated
- 1 cup vegetable stock
- ½ cup cream
- 3 tbsp. herbs de Provence
- Sea salt and freshly ground black pepper

Sauté the vegetables in some butter and olive oil, add the stock, herbs and let simmer to reduce for 10-15 min. Add the cream and reduce for 5-10 minutes more. Carefully lower the snapper into the pot and let it simmer on low heat for a few minutes until cooked. Add salt and pepper to taste.

# Garlic Shrimp

### Serves 4-6

- 1 ½ lbs. raw shrimp, rinsed and cleaned
- 5 cloves garlic, chopped
- 3 tbsp. butter
- 3 tsp. sea salt

Peel the shrimp but leave the tail on. Melt the butter in a skillet and add the garlic, being careful not to sauté on too high heat as the garlic burns easily. Place the shrimp in a row with some space in between so you can turn them individually. After a minute or so, turn each shrimp to cook the other side. After another minute, make a quick shake of the pan to blend the flavors and pour the contents in a serving bowl. Garnish with chopped fresh parsley.

# Shrimp Stir-Fry

### Serves 4-6

- 1½ lbs. cooked bay shrimp
- 6 assorted mini peppers (yellow, orange, red), pith removed, finely sliced
- 1 fennel, sliced
- ½ onion, sliced
- 3 cloves garlic, chopped
- Juice of 2 limes
- 1 bunch fresh basil, chopped
- Sea salt and freshly ground black pepper

You can use the recipe above to cook the shrimp if you like, or simply steam them for a few minutes. Start by sautéing the vegetables in some oil until they are soft. Add the garlic after a few minutes. After an additional 2 min., add the shrimp (they are just to be heated as they will turn rubbery very easily ); add the basil, lime juice, salt and pepper. Serve immediately.

# Crab Cakes

## Serves 4-6

- 1 lb. lump crab meat, slightly separated
- 5 scallions, finely chopped
- 1 jalapeno, seeded and minced
- 2 tbsp. fresh lemon juice
- ½ cup mayonnaise
- 2 tbsp. fresh cilantro, finely chopped
- ½ cup panko bread crumbs
- 1 tsp. sea salt
- ½ tsp. freshly ground black pepper
- 1-2 eggs, whisked
- Canola oil A/N

Combine the scallions, jalapeno, lemon juice, mayonnaise, cilantro, bread crumbs, salt and pepper. Let sit for 2 min. Fold in the eggs; the mixture should be fairly thick. Add in the crab and combine using your fingers. Test fry a small piece of mixture to check for seasoning. Form the mixture into 6-10 cakes with a ½ inch edge on the side.

Cover and refrigerate for 30 min. In a skillet, heat the oil until shimmering. Add the crab cakes and cook over moderate heat for about 3 min. on each side until browned. Perfectly served with the spicy chipotle mayo or roasted pepper sauce.

# Healthy Recipes for Children

We all know how hard it can sometimes be to get children to eat. They have a way of being very specific and uncompromising in their choices. A great way to get them to eat is to allow them to be involved in the process. Let them participate in the preparation and serving of the food. Chances are, once they associate the fun of having prepared the food and also know exactly what is in it, they are far more likely to want to try it. In addition, they have benefited from spending some quality time with you! Here are some healthy, tasty and easy recipes that will make the cooking and eating a joy for all involved.

# Breakfast and Snacks

## Power Cereal

**Serves 4**

- 1 cup homemade granola (See index.)
- ½ cup strawberries, sliced
- 1 cup milk, or plain yogurt
- 2 tbsp. raw honey

In two small bowls, divide the granola, add the strawberries and top with a drizzle of honey. Pour in the milk, stick in a spoon and it is ready to give your child a healthy, energetic jump-start to the day!

## Razz-berry Pancakes

**Serves 2-3**

- ¾ cup whole-wheat flour
- ½ cup raspberries, halved
- 1 whole egg
- ¾ cup milk
- 1 tbsp. butter
- 1 tbsp. brown sugar
- 1 tsp. baking powder
- ½ tsp. sea salt

In a bowl, mix the flour, sugar, baking powder and salt. Melt the butter on low heat in a saucepan. Whisk the egg with the milk and melted butter, then add the flour mixture while whisking until it is blended. Add some more butter to your saucepan and put it on medium heat until the butter starts to bubble.

Use a ladle to just about cover the bottom of the saucepan with the batter, add some raspberries on top and flip them over once with a spatula when small bubbles start to appear. Cook one minute on the other side, and then fold each pancake in half before taking it out of the pan.

# Tropical Fruity Skewers

## Serves 2-4

- 1 banana, sliced in ½ inch pieces
- 1 apple, peeled and cut in small cubes
- 1 cup pineapple chunks
- 1 cup honey melon, cut into ½ inch cubes
- 2 whole eggs
- 1 tbsp. water
- ½ cup shredded coconut
- 4 wooden skewers, soaked in water

Preheat the oven to 400°F. Prepare the fruit and thread each piece on the skewers in whatever order you like. Slightly beat the eggs and water with a fork and roll the skewers in the egg, followed by rolling each piece in the shredded coconut.

Repeat the process of 'double dipping' the fruit in the egg and coconut then place them in a baking dish. Bake in the oven for about 15 min. until golden brown. They are hot at this point so let them rest for a while before serving.

# Berry-licious Muffins

## Serves 12

- 1 cup spelt flour
- 1 cup oatmeal
- 1 cup blueberries, rinsed
- ¼ cup canola oil
- 1 whole egg
- 1 cup whole milk
- 3 tbsp. flax seeds
- 2 tbsp. brown sugar
- 4 tsp. baking powder
- 1 tsp. sea salt

Preheat the oven to 400°F. Mix the flour, oatmeal, sugar, salt, baking powder and flax seeds in a bowl; add the blueberries. In another bowl, beat the egg slightly and add the milk and canola oil.

Add the mixed dry ingredients to the egg batter and fold to blend, being careful not to stir too much. Butter a muffin tin and fill each cup about 2/3 of the way up and bake in the oven for about 20 min. When lightly browned, test by sticking in a toothpick in the middle of one of the muffins; if done, the toothpick will come out 'dry'. When ready, let them cool on a wire rack.

## Strawberry Preserves

**Serves 4-6**

- 2 cups strawberries, sliced
- 4 tbsp. raw honey
- 1 tbsp. lemon juice

In a small saucepan, let the strawberries and honey simmer on low heat for 20 min. until soft. Add the lemon juice, let cool, and store in the fridge. Use on granola, bread or oatmeal.

## Nutty Vegetables

**Serves 2-4**

- 1 large carrot
- 3 celery sticks
- 1 red pepper
- ½ cup almond or cashew nut butter

Rinse the vegetables and slice them into thin sticks about 3 inches long and ¼ inch thick. Put the nut butter in a small bowl and place it in the middle of a large plate. Evenly spread the vegetables on the plate around the bowl and it is ready to dip away.

# Dinners

# Quesadillas

## Serves 2-4

- 1 can tomato sauce
- 1 tomato, chopped
- 1 yellow onion, finely chopped
- 2 tbsp. fresh lime juice
- 3 tbsp. fresh chopped cilantro
- 2 cloves garlic, minced
- 1 cup diced chicken breast
- ½ cup shredded jack cheese
- 4 corn tortillas
- Olive oil in cooking spray container

Sauté the onions and garlic on low heat until lightly caramelized. Meanwhile, blend the tomato sauce, tomato, lime juice and cilantro and set aside. Brown off the chicken in another skillet with some olive oil and put aside into a separate bowl. Spray a large skillet with some olive oil and keep at medium heat. Assemble the quesadilla by using one corn tortilla and add the ingredients in the following order; salsa, chicken, onions, cheese then put another tortilla on top.

Repeat with the remaining ingredients. Place in skillet and when the bottom of the tortilla starts to brown, turn it over, being careful not to drop the contents from the sides. Alternately, they can be placed on a baking tray and baked in the oven for 10 min. at 350°F. Slice into quarters, then eights and serve.

# Sausage and Potato Hash

## Serves 4-6

- 4 cups cooked potatoes, diced
- 1 yellow onion, chopped
- 4 mild sausages
- 3 tbsp. butter
- 3 tbsp. whole wheat flour
- 1 ¼ cup whole milk
- 1 ½ cup shredded cheddar cheese

Preheat the oven to 375°F. Butter a wide baking dish; add the potatoes, onions and sausages. In a small saucepan, melt the butter and mix in the flour. Add the milk while stirring and keep heating and stirring until it thickens. Turn off the heat and stir in the cheese. Pour everything into your casserole and sprinkle some cheese on top. Bake in the oven for 20-30 min.

# Macaroni and Cheese Gratin

## Serves 4-6

- 3 cups elbow macaroni
- 1 cup whole milk
- 1 cup heavy whipping cream
- 2 tbsp. whole wheat
- 2 tbsp. butter
- ¾ cup shredded cheddar cheese
- 1 tsp. ground nutmeg
- 2 tsp. sea salt
- 2 tsp. freshly ground freshly ground black pepper

An all-time favorite classic. Preheat the oven to 375°F. Cook the macaroni slightly less than directed on the packet (about 6-7 min.) In a saucepan, melt the butter carefully and stir in the flour. Add the milk and cream while whisking and bring to a light simmer. After simmering for about 10-15 min. and thickened, turn off the heat and add the salt, pepper, nutmeg and ½ cup of cheese.

Blend the macaroni and sauce together in the saucepan and transfer to a flat and wide baking dish. Sprinkle the rest of the cheese on top and bake in the oven for 20 min. until the cheese turns golden brown.

# Fish Fingers

## Serves 4

- 1 lb. cod fillet or another firm white fish
- 2 whole eggs
- 1 tbsp. water
- ½ cup panko breadcrumbs
- ½ cup spelt flour
- 4 tbsp. butter
- 4 tbsp. olive oil
- Sea salt and freshly ground black pepper

Cut the fish into rectangular logs 2-2 ½ inches long and 1/2 -1 inch thick. Using a fork, slightly beat the eggs with the water. Mix the flour and breadcrumbs and add the salt and pepper. Roll the fish fingers in the mixed egg and then in the flour mix.

Repeat the process one more time and set the dipped fish fingers aside. Heat a large skillet and add the oil and butter. When the butter turns nut colored, begin sautéing the fish fingers on all sides. They are done when they turn golden brown. Serve with mashed potatoes or rice.

# Chicken Kebabs

## Serves 4

- 2 chicken breasts
- 2 zucchini
- 1 yellow pepper
- 1 cup cherry tomatoes
- 1 cup mushrooms (optional)
- Olive oil
- Sea salt and pepper

Soak 6 wooden skewers in water for 30 min. or use metal skewers. Preheat oven to 375°F. Cut chicken breasts into cubes (about 1 inch thick). Cut the zucchinis and peppers into 1-inch rounds. Thread the ingredients onto the skewers in the following order; pepper, mushroom, chicken, zucchini then tomato.

Brush the kebabs with oil. Sprinkle with salt and pepper. Bake until the veggies are tender and chicken is cooked through, about 20 min. They can also be grilled; just make sure the chicken is cooked through. Serve with whole grain pasta.

# Butterfly Casserole

## Serves 4-6

- 1 lb. ground beef or turkey
- 2 cups bowtie pasta (farfalle), uncooked
- 1 can chopped tomatoes
- 1 ½ cups water
- 1 corn on the cob
- ½ cup barbecue sauce
- Sea salt and freshly ground black pepper

In a large skillet, brown the beef (or turkey) on high heat. With a knife, slice the corn off the cob and stir the kernels in with the pasta, tomatoes, water, and barbecue sauce and bring to a boil. Reduce heat to low, cover and simmer 15 to 20 min. or until pasta is tender, stirring occasionally. Add the beef to the sauce and add salt and pepper to taste.

# The Mighty Ham Stew

## Serves 4-6

- 2 cups diced ham cubes
- 1 cup salsa
- 1 cup vegetable stock
- 1 can kidney beans, drained
- 1 medium onion, chopped
- ½ cup chopped parsley

Combine all the ingredients in a large soup pot. Bring to a boil, then reduce the heat and simmer for 5 to 10 minutes. Serve with rice, pasta or potatoes.

# Potato Pancakes

## Serves 4

- 2 cups cold mashed potatoes or cold boiled potatoes
- ½ cup whole wheat flour
- ½ cup whole milk
- 2 whole eggs
- 3 tbsp. butter
- 1 tsp. sea salt

Mash the potatoes (if they are not mashed already, leftover mash works great here) and mix in the flour. In a separate bowl, mix the milk with the eggs and salt; add the potatoes. Form small pancakes about 2 inches wide and sauté in a skillet with the butter.

# The Best Alfredo

## Serves 4-6

- 2 tbsp. butter
- 3 cloves garlic, minced
- 1 cup heavy whipping cream
- ½-1 cup grated Parmesan
- Sea salt and freshly ground black pepper

Add the butter to a sauce pot on low heat. Add the garlic and cook very gently until aromatic. Whisk in the cream and let simmer to reduce 5-10 min. Add the cheese while whisking and simmer until dissolved and thickened, about 5 min. Add salt and pepper to taste and serve with your favorite pasta

# Easy Sausage 'Gumbo'

## Serves 4-6

- 4 mild Italian chicken sausages
- 1 corn on the cob
- 1 large yellow onion, chopped
- 2 cloves garlic, chopped
- 1 large can whole tomatoes
- 1 small can chopped tomatoes
- ½ cup (1 tub) crème fraiche
- ¼ cup heavy whipping cream
- 2 tbsp. butter
- 2 tbsp. olive oil
- 2 tbsp. dried Italian herbs
- Sea salt and freshly ground black pepper to taste.

Slice the chorizo diagonally into 1/8-inch slices. Brown the sausages in a large skillet using some of the butter and oil; transfer them to a large stock pot. In the same skillet, add some more butter and oil and sauté the onions and garlic, then add them to the pot with the chorizo. Turn the heat on low for the stockpot, cut the corn off the cob and add the kernels to the pot with the tomatoes. Let simmer for 10 min.

Add the crème fraiche and whipping cream and herbs. Let simmer for another 5-10 min., then add the shrimp and wait just a couple more minutes before serving. Add salt and pepper to taste.

# Gorgonzola Alfredo

## Serves 4-6

- 1 cup Black Forest ham, diced
- ½-1 cup whole milk
- ½ cup heavy whipping cream
- ½ cup crumbled Gorgonzola cheese
- ½ cup green peas
- 1 clove garlic, chopped
- 2 tbsp. spelt flour
- 2 tbsp. butter
- Sea salt and freshly ground black pepper
- 1 packet whole grain linguine

Add the butter to a large skillet and begin browning off the ham cubes. When they have a nice color, add the garlic and stir for about a minute. Whisk the flour with the butter and ham. Pour in the milk first while whisking, making sure all the flour dissolves and then add the cream. Let simmer for 10 min., stirring occasionally and cooking the pasta at the same time.

Add the peas, wait for 2 min., add the cheese and turn off the heat. Add salt and pepper to taste. Drain the pasta and blend it in with the sauce.

# Desserts

We are all up for something sweet from time to time, and that is ok. It is important to treat yourself now and then. Having a dessert after a meal instead of by itself minimizes the harmful effect of the sugar. In addition to when and with what you have sugar, it is also very important to consider the quality and source of the raw ingredients. Good alternatives to white sugar are rapadura (See sources.), brown sugar, maple sugar, agave nectar and raw honey.

# Lavender and Honey Ice Cream

### Serves 4-6

- 2 cups whole milk
- ½ cup honey
- ½ vanilla bean
- 2 tbsp. dried lavender
- ¼ cup sugar
- 6 egg yolks
- ½ tsp. salt
- 1 ¼ cup whipping cream

Combine the milk, honey, lavender and vanilla bean in a sauce pan and let come to a simmer. Simmer until the honey has dissolved, scrape the seeds from the vanilla bean and add both bean and seeds to the pan.

Remove from heat, cover and let sit for an hour for the flavors to combine, then strain. Using a standing mixer, whisk the egg yolks with the sugar until pale and fluffy. Mix in flour and salt. Whisk in the milk and place in a clean pot.

Reheat the mixture while using a spatula, stirring constantly. Be careful that the mixture does not boil. Remove from heat, let cool slightly and mix in the cream. Chill in the refrigerator until cold; transfer the mixture to an ice cream maker and freeze according to the instructions.

# Red Wine Poached Pear

### Serves 4-6

- 4 d'Anjou pears
- 4 cups red wine
- 1 cup sugar
- 1 vanilla bean
- 1 cinnamon stick
- 5 star anise
- Water A/N

In a medium pot, add the wine, sugar, cinnamon stick and star anise. Split the vanilla bean lengthwise, scrape out the seeds and add both the bean and seeds to the pot. Let come to a light simmer. Peel the pears, cut them lengthwise and scoop out the core with a melon baller.

Add the pears to the pot and fill up with water until just covered. Let simmer covered until very soft, about 30 min. Transfer the pears and liquid to a glass container and refrigerate for 4 hours.

The pears will keep for up to 5 days in the liquid. Alternately, you can peel the pear only and cook whole. Just scoop out the core after cooling down with a melon baller and cut gently from the top, cutting through a diagonal all the way through the bottom.

# Strawberry and Banana Crunch

### Serves 6-8

For the dough:
- 2 cups flour
- 1 ½ sticks (6 oz.) butter, cut into 1/8 inch cubes
- ½ cup brown sugar
- 1 tsp. sea salt

For the filling:
- 2 cups strawberries, sliced
- 3 fresh bananas
- 1 cup pecans, chopped
- ½ cup honey

For the chocolate sauce:
- 1.75 oz. dark chocolate
- 50 g butter
- ¾ cup milk
- 2 tbsp. flour
- 1 tbsp. instant or strong coffee
- 1 tbsp. honey

Make the dough from the flour, butter and sugar by molding all ingredients with your hands, forming a ball; cover and keep it in the fridge until needed. Slice the strawberries and bananas in a buttered tart pan; make a layer of the bananas followed by the strawberries. Sprinkle the chopped pecans on top and drizzle the honey over the nuts.

Spread the dough in small crumbles over the fruit and nuts and bake in the oven at 350°F for 25-30 min. Meanwhile, make the chocolate sauce by first melting the butter, mixing in the flour completely, adding the milk and slowly heating up.

When almost boiling, add the dark chocolate to melt; as soon as it is melted, add the coffee and honey and simmer while stirring for a few minutes until thickened. Taste to see if more honey is needed.

# Blueberry Tart

### Serves 10-16

For tart shell:
- 4 oz. butter, (1 stick), cut into 1/8 inch cubes
- 2 oz. sugar
- 1 egg yolk
- 5 oz. flour
- 2 tbsp. ice water

For blueberry filling:
- 2 cups blueberries
- ½ cup powdered sugar
- 2 tbsp. lemon juice
- 1-2 oz. corn starch

Preheat the oven to 350°F. To make the tart shell, combine the flour and sugar in a stand mixer. Run on low speed, adding the butter, until a coarse meal forms. Add the egg yolk and water little by little until a moist clump forms. Press the dough into a ball then form a thin disc. Cover with plastic wrap and chill for 30 min.

Meanwhile, make the filling by combining all ingredients in a sauce pot and cooking over medium heat, stirring occasionally. When the blueberries start to soften and the juice starts to thicken, remove the pot from the heat and set aside. Roll out the dough and place in an 8 inch tart pan with removable edge.

Poke some holes halfway through the dough with a fork, line with plastic wrap and fill the crust with dried beans. Fold the plastic wrap over the beans, put the tart shell in the middle of the oven and bake for about 7 min. until the edges turn somewhat white and puffy.

Take it out of the oven and remove the plastic wrap and beans. Bake for another 10-15 min. until fully cooked and the edges are light brown. Fill the tart crust with the blueberry filling and bake for another 5 min. Let cool completely on a wire rack.

# Mom's Carrot Cake

## Serves 6-8

For the cake:
- 1 ¾ cup peeled and grated carrots
- 1 ¼ cups canola oil
- 1 ½ cups sugar
- 3 eggs
- 1 ¾ cups all-purpose flour
- 1 tsp. baking powder
- 1 tsp. baking soda
- ½ tsp. salt
- ½ tsp. nutmeg
- 1 tsp. cinnamon
- ½ cups walnuts, coarsely chopped

For the icing:
- 8 oz. butter, melted and cooled
- 8 oz. Philadelphia cream cheese, at room temperature
- 1 ¼ cups powder sugar
- 2 tsp. vanilla extract
- Juice and zest of 1 lemon

Preheat the oven to 375°F. Using a standing mixer, whisk the sugar with the oil until pale white and fluffy. Add the carrots followed by the eggs one at a time, whisking in between. Combine all the dry ingredients and add to the mixture.

Lastly, fold in the walnuts. Butter and flour a 12 inch cake pan with removable edges and pour in the batter. Bake the cake for about 45 min. until a tester comes out clean when pierced through the center. Let cool on wire rack. Meanwhile, whisk all ingredients for the icing, combining the butter and Philadelphia first, and then sifting in the sugar followed by the vanilla extract and lemon juice and zest. Spread the icing over the cake when it's fully cooled and let sit in a cool place for a while to stiffen slightly.

# Mango sorbet

## Serves 4-6

- 2 ripe mangoes, peeled and chopped
- ½ cup sugar
- Water A/N
- 1 cup pineapple or mango juice
- ½ cup coconut milk
- 3 tbsp. fresh lime juice

Put the sugar in a small sauce pan and add water until the sugar resembles wet sand. Cover and turn on a medium heat. When boiling, remove the lid and simmer for about 5 min.

Remove from heat and transfer to a mixing bowl and chill. In a blender, combine the remaining ingredients and puree until smooth. With the motor running, add the sugar syrup in a slow stream until fully combined. Freeze in an ice cream maker according to the instructions, place in a glass container and transfer to the freezer.

# Grand Marnier-Infused Berries with Lime Zest

**Serves 4**

- ½ cup blueberries
- ½ cup raspberries
- ½ cup strawberries, cut into ¼ inch dice
- ¼ cup Grand Marnier
- Zest of 1 lime
- ½ cup powder sugar
- 1 tsp. vanilla

Toss all ingredients in a bowl and let macerate for 20-30 min. in the refrigerator. Serve with ice cream in a martini glass and garnish with more lime zest and a mint leaf.

# Caramel Pecan Tart

**Serves 6-8**

For the pie crust:
- 2 ¼ cups all-purpose flour
- ¼ cup sugar
- ¼ tsp. sea salt
- 2 sticks unsalted butter
- ¼ cup ice water

For the pecan filling:
- 2 cups pecan halves
- 3 eggs
- ½ cup packed brown sugar
- 3 tbsp. butter, melted
- ¾ cup dark corn syrup
- 2 tbsp. bourbon
- ¼ tsp. salt
- 1 tsp. vanilla extract

To make the pie crust, combine the dry ingredients and, using a box grater, grate the butter into the flour. Combine with your hands until the butter is evenly dispersed into pea-sized balls. Add the water and knead until a dough forms. Add more water if it's too dry. Flatten into a disc, wrap in plastic and place in the refrigerator for 30 min. Preheat the oven to 375°F. Roll out the dough using some flour and place in a 12 inch tart round with removable edge. Poke small holes halfway through the dough with a fork and line with plastic film. Pour dry beans into the crust and fold the plastic over. Bake until the edges are somewhat white and puffy, about 7-10 min.

Remove the plastic and beans and bake until the bottom is somewhat white and edges light brown. Meanwhile, using an electric mixer, beat the eggs and sugar until light and fluffy. Beat in the butter, bourbon, vanilla, and salt. Fold in the pecans. Pour the batter into the pie crust and bake until it sets and the edges are golden brown, about 25-30 min. Cool on a rack for an hour before serving.

# Apple
## Crumble

### Serves 6-8

For the filling:
- 5-6 soft apples like Red Delicious or Pink Lady
- 4 tbsp. ground cinnamon
- 4 tbsp. brown sugar or honey

For the crumble:
- 1 cup oats
- 1 cup whole-wheat or spelt flour
- 1 stick (4 oz.) butter, cold
- Grated zest of 1 lemon
- 2 tsp. ground ginger
- 1 tsp. sea salt

Preheat the oven to 375°F. Make the crumble by mixing the oats, flour, lemon peel and ginger. Cut 1/8 inch chunks of the butter and mix it with your hands with the flour and oats; it is good if it is a little lumpy and coarse. Form into a ball, cover and place in the fridge while preparing the apples. Peel the apples, core and cut in fairly thin wedges.

Place them in a buttered 9-inch pie form, add the sugar and cinnamon and blend it with your hands. Spread the crumble evenly over the apples. Bake in the middle of the oven for 20-25 min. until the top starts to brown and the apples get soft.

Serve with organic vanilla ice cream or vanilla custard.

# Chocolate Cake

**Serves 6-8**

- 4 whole eggs
- 1 ¾ cups brown sugar
- 1 cup flour
- ½ tbsp. cacao
- 2 tsp. vanilla extract
- 2 tbsp. strong coffee or instant
- About 2 sticks (8 oz.) of butter
- 200 g dark chocolate, chopped
- ½ cup walnuts, chopped

Melt the butter and chocolate over a double boiler, but keep some chopped chocolate for garnish. When melted, add the coffee and vanilla extract and let cool slightly. Whisk the eggs and sugar until fluffy and whisk in the flour and cacao.

Add the chocolate while stirring and pour the batter into a buttered and floured round baking dish with removable edges. Sprinkle some crushed chocolate and the walnuts on top and bake at 350°F for 45 min., until almost cooked through. Check the middle with a thin stick; it should be a little soft for a moist consistency. Let cool a bit and serve with a spoonful of whipped cream.

# Coconut and Almond Panna Cotta

**Serves 4-6**

For the panna cotta:
- 1 cup cream
- ½ cup milk
- 2 egg yolks
- 2 tbsp. sugar
- 2 leaves of gelatin
- ¼ cup shredded coconut
- ¼ cup slivered almonds

For the strawberry sauce:
- 1-2 cups strawberries, sliced
- ½ cup sugar

Make the panna cotta: Soak the gelatin in cold water for at least 5 min. Put the cream, milk, egg yolks and sugar into a pot and heat carefully while stirring. When small bubbles appear, remove from the heat and let rest for a little while, then stir in the gelatin to dissolve.

Butter 4-6 small cups or glasses and add the shredded coconut into each. Pour in the cream into the cups over the coconut and garnish with some slivered almonds. Let cool in the fridge until hard, at least 4 hours. To make the strawberry sauce, heat the strawberries in a pot with the sugar until dissolved; simmer for 5-10 min. Serve the sauce hot over the panna cotta.

# Yogurt and Berries

### Serves 4-6

- 1 cup Greek yogurt or vanilla ice cream
- 1½ cups mixed berries, blueberries, raspberries and strawberries
- ½ cup maple sugar or syrup
- 4 tbsp. grated dark chocolate (optional)
- 4 tbsp. dark rum (optional)

Spoon half of the yogurt into martini glasses or small bowls; add the mixed berries and the maple sugar, followed by the rest of the yogurt. Top off with a drizzle of rum and a sprinkle of chocolate.

---

# Tropical Delight

### Serves 6-8

- 1 cup almonds or almond meal
- 1 cup spelt flour
- ½ cup butter or coconut oil
- ½ cup maple sugar or rapadura
- 2 cups whipped cream
- 3-4 fresh bananas
- ¾ cup dried unsweetened coconut meat
- 1 tsp. vanilla extract
- ½ tsp. sea salt

Pour the almonds into a food processor and grind into a meal/flour consistency; add the remaining ingredients except bananas and cream and pulse until well-blended.

Butter a 10-inch tart pan and press the dough in so it covers the bottom of the pan and up onto the edges as well. Bake at 300°F for 45 min. Let cool, slice over the bananas and top off with the whipped cream.

# Breakfast

Breakfast is a vastly de-prioritized meal, relative to its importance. Since you have not eaten for the entire night, your blood sugar is going to drop fast if you start moving without eating. It is also in the morning that we set the foundation of energy; with a good morning meal, you can rely on having sustained energy throughout the entire day. The body, especially the brain, requires a great deal of energy to function optimally. That energy is obtained from food. In addition, for example, if you only have coffee and no breakfast in the morning, your blood sugar level will plummet and when it does, your body will start to utilize the quickest available energy source.

Unlike what you might expect or hope, that source is NOT the fat. Fat needs to be burned in a slow specific process. It is the muscle protein that will be utilized first as it is the easiest and most available energy for the body. When you have lunch later in the day, you will be so starved that you are far more likely to eat an unnecessarily large portion that will not only leave you feeling sleepy and reaching for the first available coffee pot, but will also significantly increase your body's fat storage process. This is, to put it simply, due to the fact that the body has been in starvation mode for so long, that when it finally does get food, it will store it mostly as fat because of a survival mechanism that activates when the body has drawn from stored energy and does not know when it will get fed again. Here are a few wholesome quick recipes that will jumpstart your day and give you the energy to be at your best.

# Oatmeal with Walnuts and Banana

### Serves 2-4

- 2 cups oats
- 2 cups filtered water
- 2 cups whole milk
- 1 cinnamon stick
- 3 tbsp. ground flax seeds
- ¾ cup banana, sliced
- ¾ cup walnuts, coarsely chopped
- 1 tsp. sea salt

Start by heating a stainless steel pot and pouring in the oats. After they have roasted for a short while (be careful not to burn the oats), add the water and milk. Add the nuts, and salt and let simmer for 10 min., stirring occasionally. Stir in the flax seeds towards the end and serve with milk and the sliced bananas on top with a sprinkle of cinnamon. The bananas can be replaced with ½ of a freshly grated apple.

# Oatmeal with Goji Berries

### Serves 2-4

- 2 cups oats
- 2 cups filtered water
- 2 cups whole milk
- 1 cinnamon stick
- 3 tbsp. ground flax seeds
- ½ cup goji berries
- 1 tsp. sea salt

Use the above recipe to make the oatmeal but add the goji berries instead. This is a bowl of pure energy and nutrients.

# Oatmeal with Apricots and Almonds

### Serves 2-4

- 2 cups oats
- 2 cups filtered water
- 2 cups whole milk
- 1 cinnamon stick
- 3 tbsp. ground flax seeds
- ¾ cup dried sliced apricots
- ¾ cup blanched almonds, slivered
- 1 tsp. sea salt

As you will see, there are endless ways to vary your oatmeal. For instance, if you are lactose intolerant, use water instead of milk and soy, almond or rice milk when serving. Start by heating a stainless steel pot and putting in the oats. After they have 'roasted' gently for a short while (being careful not to burn them), add the water and milk. Stir, then add the nuts, apricots and spices and let simmer for 10 min., stirring occasionally. Towards the end, mix in the flax seeds with the oats and serve with milk and a sprinkle of cinnamon.

# Scrambled Eggs

### Serves 2

- 4 whole eggs
- 1/2 cup whole milk
- A pinch of sea salt
- 1 tbsp. olive oil

It is very easy to make delicious, nourishing scrambled eggs. Thoroughly whisk the eggs, milk and salt. In a pot, gently heat the olive oil and put the eggs in before it is too hot. Use a flat or scraping spatula to scrape the eggs off the bottom, stirring occasionally to cook. As soon as they turn somewhat firm, remove the eggs from the heat to maintain their softness and serve immediately.

# Omelet

## Serves 1

- 2 whole eggs
- 2 tbsp. water or milk
- A pinch of sea salt
- ½ tbsp. butter

In a small bowl, mix the eggs with the water and salt. Heat a small skillet with the butter and wait until bubbles subside. Add the mixture when the skillet is hot; use a spatula to lift one side of the egg that has hardened and tilt the pan so that the remaining batter falls into the bare skillet section. When all of the egg is hardened, take off the heat and using the spatula, roll off the pan onto a plate.

In addition to this base recipe, there are many variations that can be made. Simply add tomato, green peppers or mushrooms to the pan before pouring in the egg batter to create variety.

# Homemade Raw Protein Bar

## Serves 1

- 1 cup oats
- 1 cup whole milk
- 1 tbsp. molasses or raw honey
- 4 tbsp. almond butter
- 4 tbsp. flax seeds, ground
- 1 ½ cups ProTargo™ protein powder, or other whey protein powder

Pour the oats into a bowl and blend in the protein powder, flax seeds and salt. Spoon in the almond butter, molasses (or honey) and milk, then work the batter with your hands.

Put it all on a plate and shape into a rectangle, cover and let it rest in the fridge for 20 min. Cut the hardened bar in 4 or 5 pieces and wrap individually. Store them cold.

# Muesli (granola)

### Serves 10-12

- 4 cups oats
- ½ cup dried apricots, sliced
- ½ cup dried mango, sliced
- ½ cup dried pineapple
- ½ cup coconut, shredded
- 1 cup raw mixed nuts, coarsely chopped
- 1 tbsp. cinnamon
- ½ tbsp. cardamom
- 3 tbsp. canola oil
- ½ cup flax seeds
- 1 vanilla pod, cut lengthwise

Spread all ingredients except the fruit and vanilla on a baking tray. Put it in the center of the oven at 420°F and roast for 5 min. Stir, then roast for another 5-10 min. until slightly brown and aromatic. Let it cool and add the fruit and vanilla and store in an airtight container. Enjoy with yogurt or milk as a great start of the day.

# Yogurt with Fresh Fruit and Nuts

### Serves 1

- 1 cup whole milk or yogurt
- ½ apple, coarsely chopped
- 1 handful walnuts, soaked
- 2 tbsp. flaxseeds
- 2 tbsp. cinnamon

Place the apples, nuts, flaxseeds and cinnamon in bowl, blend a little then add in the yogurt.

# Breakfast Quinoa

**Serves 2-4**

- 3 cups quinoa flakes or cooked quinoa
- ½ cup walnuts and pecans, coarsely chopped
- 1 cup apple juice
- 1 cup raisins
- 1 tbsp. grated lemon zest (optional)
- 1 cinnamon stick

Gently sauté the raisins, lemon zest and cinnamon in the apple juice for 3-5 min. Add the quinoa flakes and nuts and turn off the heat. Let sit for a few minutes, until liquid is absorbed.

---

# Baked Protein Bar

**Gives 10-12 pieces**

- 1 cup oats
- 1 cup almond meal
- 1 ½ cups ProTargo™ protein powder, or other whey protein powder
- ½ cup slivered almonds
- ½ cup whole milk
- 3 whole eggs
- 3 tbsp. ground flax seeds
- 3 tbsp. dark amber maple syrup
- 2 tsp. sea salt
- 1 tsp. baking soda

Preheat the oven to 375°F. Start by mixing the oats, protein powder, almond meal, flax seeds, baking soda and salt in a bowl. In another bowl, whisk the eggs with the milk and the maple syrup. Add the eggs and milk to the bowl with the protein and oats. Whisk a little and pour the batter into a buttered square pan (about 9 x 9).

Sprinkle the almonds on top and bake in the middle of the oven for 25-30 min., checking the middle with a thin stick to make sure it is ready. Let it cool in the pan for a while then cut it into 1 x 4 inch bars. Store them in the fridge.

# Spanish Omelet

## Serves 4

- 5 whole eggs
- 4 tbsp. milk or cream
- A pinch of sea salt
- ½ tbsp. butter
- 1 small onion, finely chopped
- ½ red pepper, finely chopped
- 1 medium tomato, coarsely chopped
- 2 small cooked cold potatoes (optional)
- A few slices of ham
- 2 tsp. dried basil or oregano
- ½ cup grated Parmesan or feta cheese

Preheat the broiler in the oven. In a small bowl, mix the eggs with the cream and salt. Heat a small skillet with the butter and wait until bubbles subside. Add the onions first and sauté for a little, add the peppers and ham, sauté for 2 min. and lastly add the tomatoes.

Add the potatoes, sprinkle over the cheese and add the eggs. Lower the heat and cook for a few minutes, then transfer the pan to the oven to brown the top. Be careful not to burn it, depending on how hot your broiler is. Let rest for a few minutes before cutting into it.

# Sources

### Salt:

Use unrefined sea salt that is a slightly gray in color since it contains up to 80 trace minerals. This is of great benefit to your body, aiding the nutritional absorption of other minerals, as well as hydrating your cells from the inside out. The best brands are Celtic sea salt from France (selinanaturally.com) or Himalayan pink salt. Herbamare herbal salt is another great tasting, nutritious salt that can be purchased at health food stores or at www.rapunzel.com.

### Stocks:

A vegetable or chicken stock is the easiest way to enhance the nutritional value and flavor of your dish. You can make your own vegetable stock by cooking onions, carrots and celery along with filtered water and sea salt for about an hour and then straining. Add a whole chicken for chicken stock and simmer for up to 8 hours, then strain. Otherwise, there are great ready-made stocks nowadays; just make sure they are certified organic (www.imaginefoods.com). There are also great vegetable stock cubes. The best ones I have found are also from Rapunzel (www.rapunzel.com) which also carries high quality oils and other great products.

### Oils:

Make sure you get high quality, unprocessed vegetable oils since these are healthiest for you. Avoid poor quality margarine and shortening since their molecular structures actually resemble plastic rather than food. A good resource to purchase great quality oils is www.radiantlifecatalog.com.

### Dairy:

It is especially important to buy organic dairy products since many of the pesticides and hormones used in the raising of the animals are stored in the fat of dairy. This animal fat is actually healthy for you, if it is of high quality and is consumed in moderate amounts. In addition, conventionally farmed dairy is so heavily processed that almost no life is left in it. Crème fraiche is a cultured cream, similar to sour cream and is usually available in the dairy section. Good brands are Horizon (www.horizondairy.com) and Organic Valley. (www.organicvalley.coop).

### Breads:

Try to avoid 'enriched' white flour breads as these are very processed and lack the nutrition the body needs. Choose instead wholesome wholegrain, sourdough, rye breads, pumpernickel, or sprouted grain (alvaradostreetbakery.com).

### Bulk Commodity:

There is great benefit in buying stock items like rice, quinoa, oats, lentils and nuts in bulk, not only because it is cheaper but also because they often come from your local farmer. Store it in airtight glass containers.

## Conversion charts
Weights and measures have been rounded up or down slightly to make measuring easier.

*Weight equivalents*

| American | Metric | Imperial |
|---|---|---|
| 1 teaspoon (tsp.) | 5 ml | |
| 1 tablespoon (tbsp.) | 15ml | |
| ¼ cup | 60 ml | 2 fl. oz. |
| ⅓ cup | 75 ml | 2 ½ fl. oz. |
| ½ cup | 125 ml | 4 fl. oz. |
| ⅔ cup | 150 ml | 5 fl. oz. |
| ¾ cup | 175 ml | 6 fl. oz. |
| 1 cup | 250 ml | 8 fl. oz. |

*Weight equivalents*

| Imperial | Metric | Inches | Cm |
|---|---|---|---|
| 1 oz. | 25g | ¼ | 5 mm |
| 2 oz. | 50g | ½ | 1 cm |
| 3oz. | 75g | ¾ | 1.5 cm |
| 4 oz. | 125g | 1 | 2.5 cm |
| 5 oz. | 150g | 2 | 5 cm |
| 6 oz. | 175g | 3 | 7 cm |
| 7 oz. | 200g | 4 | 10 cm |
| 8 oz. | 250g | 5 | 12 cm |
| 9 oz. | 275g | 6 | 15 cm |
| 10 oz. | 300g | 7 | 18 cm |
| 11 oz. | 325g | 8 | 20 cm |
| 12 oz. | 375g | 9 | 23 cm |
| 13 oz. | 400g | 10 | 25 cm |
| 14 oz. | 425g | 11 | 28 cm |
| 15 oz. | 475g | 12 | 30 cm |
| 16 oz. | 500g | | |
| 2 lbs. | 1 kg | | |

*Oven temperatures*

| Celsius | Fahrenheit | Gas |
|---|---|---|
| 65°C | 150°F | |
| 107°C | 225°F | Gas ¼ |
| 121°C | 250°F | Gas ½ |
| 135°C | 275°F | Gas 1 |
| 149°C | 300°F | Gas 2 |
| 163°C | 325°F | Gas 3 |
| 177°C | 350°F | Gas 4 |
| 191°C | 375°F | Gas 5 |
| 200°C | 390°F | Gas 6 |
| 204°C | 400°F | Gas 7 |
| 218°C | 425°F | Gas 8 |
| 230°C | 450°F | Gas 9 |
| 240°C | 475°F | Gas 10 |

# About the author

Daniel is a Le Cordon Bleu graduate and private chef, with a background in personal training and nutrition, specializing in healthy cuisine. He has more than 10 years of cooking experience and his passion for cooking and living a healthy lifestyle has inspired him to experiment in the kitchen, perfecting his skills and developing his own interesting flavor combinations and special dishes. He has a holistic approach and chooses to cook organic and eco-friendly whenever possible.

Daniel grew up in Sweden, where the traditional foods are wholesome and empowering; he was included in the kitchen since childhood and found he had a natural inclination to the craft and a great taste memory. The healthy aspect of food preparation became his focus at the young age of 15, when he also started his fitness training. He started his career by attending nutrition and fitness classes in Sweden and London, eventually getting certifications in personal training and message therapy. This led him to run his own personal training and message therapy business in London for three years in the early 2000's.

He worked for a highly respected catering company in London, managing and serving food for large and high profile events. He was part of the team that worked the 2004 Christmas dinner at Windsor Castle for Prince Charles, as well as Queen Elizabeth's staff party.

Daniel moved to Los Angeles in 2005 and received an AA from Santa Monica College. Soon after, he decided to follow his passion for food and also graduated with honors from the prestigious Le Cordon Bleu Culinary Institute of California. He is currently working as a private chef and is often asked to share his knowledge on radio shows, organic cooking workshops, blogs and panels. He is also the co-owner of NutriVision USA, a manufacturer of top quality Swedish sports and food supplements.

## Special Thanks

Noel Arias for the cover and book design.
Peggy Oei for main photography and image correction.
Bernard Belliveau for additional photography.
Sami Rusani for web solutions, ideas and support.
Nan Deyo for proof reading.
Robert Johansson for assistance and clean up.

### *Works Cited*

Chek, Paul. How to eat, move and be healthy. San Diego: 2004.
Faidon, Magkos, Fotini Arvaniti and Antonis Zampelas. "Organic food: Nutritious Food or Food For Thought, A Review of the Evidence." International Journal of Food Sciences and Nutrition vol. 54, 5 (2003): 357-371. http://libdb.smc.edu/login?url=http://search.epnet.com.libdb.smc.edu/login.aspx?direct=true&db=aph&an=10466138

Horrigan, Leo. Robert S Lawrence and Polly Walker. "How Sustainable Agriculture Can Address the Environmental and Human Health Harms of Industrial Agriculture." Environmental Health Perspectives 110 5 (2002): 445-56. http://libdb.smc.edu/login?url=http://search.epnet.com.libdb.smc.edu/login.aspx?direct=true&db=aph&an=6750413

Lea, Emma. "Food, Health, The Environment and Consumers' Dietary Choices." Nutrition and Dietetics 62 (2005): 21-25.
http://libdb.smc.edu/login?url=http://search.epnet.com.libdb.smc.edu/login.aspx?direct=true&db=aph&an=16566514

Lundegardh, Bengt. Anna Martensson. "Organically Produced Plant Foods - Evidence of Health Benefits." Soil and Plant Sci 53 (2003): 3-15.
http://libdb.smc.edu/login?url=http://search.epnet.com.libdb.smc.edu/login.aspx?direct=true&db=aph&an=9780181

Pimmentel, David, et al. "Environmental, Energetic, and Economic Comparisons of Organic and Conventional Farming Systems." BioScience 55 7 (2005): 573-82.

Riffaldi, Ricardo, et al. "Organically and Conventionally Managed Soils: Characterization of Composition." Archives of Agronomy and Soil Science 49 (2003): 349-355. http://libdb.smc.edu/login?url=http://search.epnet.com.libdb.smc.edu/login.aspx?direct=true&db=aph&an=10779922

Rivera, Rudy and Roger D. Deutch. Your Hidden Food Allergies Are Making You Fat. Rocklin: Prima Publishing, 1998. Wolcott, William and Trish Fahey. The Metabolic Typing Diet. New York: Broadway Books, 2000.

www.ingramcontent.com/pod-product-compliance
Lightning Source LLC
Chambersburg PA
CBHW040533020526
44117CB00028B/12